Through the Ages in
Palestinian Archaeology

Through the Ages in Palestinian Archaeology

An Introductory Handbook

WALTER E. RAST

Trinity Press International   Philadelphia

First Edition 1992
Trinity Press International
P.O. Box 851
Valley Forge, PA 19482

Cover design by Jim Gerhard

Library of Congress Cataloging-in-Publication Data

Rast, Walter E., 1930–
    Through the ages in Palestinian archaeology : an introductory hand-
book / Walter E. Rast.
        p.   cm.
    Includes bibliographical references and index.
    ISBN 1-56338-055-2 :
    1. Palestine—Antiquities. 2. Jordan—Antiquities. 3. Excavations (Ar-
chaeology)—Palestine. 4. Excavations (Archaeology)—Jordan. I. Title.
DS111.R27   1992
933—dc20
                                                            92-33156
                                                                CIP

Printed in the United States of America.
98 99 00   6 5 4

Contents

Illustration Credits

1.1	Expedition to the Dead Sea Plain, Jordan, R.T. Schaub and W. Rast.
1.2	Expedition to the Dead Sea Plain, Jordan, R.T. Schaub and W. Rast.
2.1	Map by J. Obermann.
2.2	Expedition to the Dead Sea Plain, Jordan, R.T. Schaub and W. Rast.
3.1	Expedition to the Dead Sea Plain, Jordan, R.T. Schaub and W. Rast.
3.2	Photo by W. Rast.
3.3	Map by J. Obermann.
4.1	D.O. Henry (reproduced from *Studies in the History and Archaeology of Jordan II*, p. 70, fig. 4).
4.2	American Schools of Oriental Research (reproduced from G.O. Rollefson, *Bulletin of the American Schools of Oriental Research Supplement 23* [1985], p. 49, fig. 10).
5.1	Israel Exploration Society (reproduced from C. Epstein, *Israel Exploration Journal 25* [1975], pl. 22.4).
5.2	Israel Exploration Society (reproduced from P. Bar-Adon, *The Cave of the Treasure*, 1980, p. 28 "crown").
5.3	Expedition to the Dead Sea Plain, Jordan, R.T. Schaub and W. Rast.
6.1	Expedition to the Dead Sea Plain, Jordan, R.T. Schaub and W. Rast.
6.2	American Schools of Oriental Research (reproduced from P. Lapp, *Bulletin of the American Schools of Oriental Research 195* [1969], p. 7, fig. 3).
6.3	P. Miroschedji (reproduced from *Yarmouth 1: Rapport sur les trois premières campagnes de fouilles à Tel Yarmouth (Israël) (1980–1982)*, p. 39, fig. 2).

Illustration Credits

6.4 American Schools of Oriental Research (reproduced from R. Cohen and W.G. Dever, *Bulletin of the American Schools of Oriental Research* 243 [1981], p. 65, fig. 8).

7.1 Photo by Lee C. Ellenberger, courtesy of The Joint Expedition to Tell Balâṭah/Shechem.

7.2 Photo courtesy of The British School of Archaeology in Jerusalem.

7.3 Institute of Archaeology, Hebrew University (reproduced from Y. Yadin and others, *Hazor I*, pl. 29:1).

7.4 Photo courtesy of The British School of Archaeology in Jerusalem.

8.1 Israel Exploration Society (reproduced from T. Dothan, *The Philistines and their Material Culture*, 1982, pl. 32 left.

8.2 W. Rast, *Taanach I*, Fig. 9.

8.3 Institute of Archaeology, Tel-Aviv University (Z. Herzog in *Beer-Sheba II*, 1984, p. 76, fig. 32).

9.1 W. Rast, *Taanach I*, figs. 46:12 and 45:7.

9.2 N. Lapp and the Taanach Publication Committee.

9.3 Israel Exploration Society (W.G. Dever in *Encyclopedia of Archaeological Excavations in the Holy Land vol. 2*, 1976, p. 436).

9.4 American Schools of Oriental Research (Y. Shiloh and D. Tarler, *Biblical Archaeologist* 49 [1986], p. 199).

10.1 Israel Exploration Society (B. Mazar in *Encyclopedia of Archaeological Excavations in the Holy Land vol. 2*, 1976, p. 582).

10.2 Institute of Archaeology, Tel-Aviv University (Drawing by G. LaGrange in D. Ussishkin, *The Conquest of Lachish by Sennacherib*, 1982, p. 124, fig. 96).

10.3 Harvard Semitic Museum (G.A. Reisner, *Israelite Ostraca from Samaria*, pl. 5, no. 21).

10.4 Photo courtesy of L. Herr and the Madaba Plains Project.

11.1 Photo courtesy of The Leon Levy Expedition to Ashkelon, Carl Andrews (excavated by Andrew Appleyard).

11.2 Institute of Archaeology, Hebrew University (Y. Yadin and others, *Hazor III-IV*, 1961, pl. 262:6, 27).

11.3 Israel Exploration Society (N. Avigad in *Encyclopedia of Archaeological Excavations in the Holy Land vol.* 4, 1978, p. 1042.

11.4 American Schools of Oriental Research (N. Lapp, *The Excavations at Araq el-Emir*, Annual of the American Schools of Oriental Research vol. 47, 1983, p. 23, no. 4).

12.1 Photo by W. Rast.

12.2 Photo by W. Rast.

12.3 Photo by W. Rast.

12.4 Israel Exploration Society (M. Magen, *Qadmoniot* 17 [1984], p. 118).

12.5 Israel Exploration Society (J. Green and Y. Tsafrir, *Qadmoniot* 16 [1983], p. 29).

13.1 American Schools of Oriental Research (E. Ulrich, *Bulletin of the American Schools of Oriental Research* 268 [1987], p. 23, no. 5).

13.2 Photo by W. Rast.

13.3 American Schools of Oriental Research (M. Piccirillo, *Biblical Archaeologist* 51 [1988], p. 213).

13.4 Photo courtesy of Eric M. Meyers.

14.1 College of Wooster Expedition to Pella (R. Smith, *Pella of the Decapolis vol. 1*, 1973, pl. 85: 281).

14.2 Photo by W. Rast.

14.3 Photo courtesy of B. MacDonald.

14.4 Photo by W. Rast.

Acknowledgments

I wish to acknowledge the generous contributions of Carol Meyers, William Dever, Eric Meyers, and James Sauer in reading the original manuscript of this book. Each made valuable suggestions to which I have given careful attention, while I alone bear the responsibility for any weaknesses that still remain. This is also an appropriate place to record my gratitude for the numerous collegial relationships I have had as a member of the American Schools of Oriental Research. There is little in this book that has not been informed in some way by associations with the many scholars in that professional organization. Also, although we see one another less frequently, contacts with colleagues in Jordan, Israel, the West Bank, Europe, Great Britain, Australia, and other countries and areas, have been a source of ongoing knowledge and insight. My appreciation is also noted here to Michael Kessler, who prepared the index. Finally, I would like to thank my brother, Harold, for encouraging me to carry through on this writing project, and for his interest in publishing it, and Laura Barrett, whose assistance from the offices of Trinity Press International has been impressively professional and always gracious.

Introduction

We are about to embark on a journey through time that will open our eyes to one of the most challenging places for archaeology anywhere in the world, the land of ancient Palestine, or, as it is known today, modern Israel, Gaza, the West Bank, and Jordan.

Few areas of the world have such an abundance of archaeological remains below the surface as does this area. And few countries have been so intensely investigated as those of this region. This is not only because ancient Palestine was the land in which the Bible was written. To be sure, the fact that this was the place where the biblical stories originated, or where the people of Israel and Jesus lived, has made it an especially important land for many people. But there is more to the archaeology of this area than these biblical connections. It has been discovered, for example, that the region of ancient Palestine is one of the most important for the history of earliest peoples of the Stone Age, and this has led a growing number of prehistorians to launch projects dealing with this aspect of the ancient land.

Other scholars have studied how the peoples of the Bronze Age in Palestine reacted to the new dynamics of urbanization found elsewhere in the Middle East. And still others have concentrated on the archaeology of early Christianity, on the Jewish community through the centuries following the New Testament, or on the emergence of the new religion of Islam and its social influences. Palestinian archaeology today includes much more than the biblical periods, despite the fact that the biblical periods continue to have their special importance.

In the archaeological remains of ancient Palestine, therefore, we encounter an embarrassment of riches. So abundant are these remains that they overwhelm us not only by their quantity, but also through the great expanse of time they cover. In addition, with the development of ever-improving techniques for retrieving evidence of the past, a single expedition today can gather enough data in several seasons of fieldwork to occupy a group of scholars for many years of study. As a result, the technical reports of expeditions, when they finally appear, are usually daunting in their detail.

Such detailed study, however, can be left to the scholars to discuss and debate. In the fruit of their intensive labors we today can enjoy for the first time a more complete picture of the history and cultures of the ancient Near East than people at any time have been able to do, even the peoples of those ancient times themselves. Not only have the buried civilizations of Egypt and Mesopotamia been resurrected through the intricate work of archaeology, but those of Turkey, Iran, Syria, and, of course, Palestine, have all been brought back from the past to enchant us as examples of the earliest societies of humankind.

In what follows, this broad picture will be traced in one area only, that of ancient Palestine. We will not pretend to cover everything. That would be impossible and, indeed, unnecessary. Numerous important sites and discoveries will be passed over, and many potentially interesting subjects will not be taken up. Like any traveler, we must pick and choose, and the objective should be to obtain something of an integrated understanding rather than a barrage of factual data that may seem diffuse and unrelated. As in any well-thought-out travel plan, some will probably want to disembark at certain points, to investigate a subject more extensively. That is the purpose of the bibliography at the end, which will guide the interested reader to further resources on a particular subject.

Readers will come at this material with varied interests. Some may prefer looking at things from an anthropological, social, or cultural perspective, while others will be especially interested in the history of the periods discussed. For those with a special interest in the Bible, the chapters dealing with the Iron Age are accompanied by suggestions for putting together the archaeological discussions with suggested biblical readings. Others who are interested in the history of religion may find the chapters dealing with the archaeology of Judaism, Christianity, and Islam to be useful.

Introduction

On our journey, therefore, we will come to know many different peoples who have lived in this ancient land over the millennia. Without realizing that their remains would one day enable people like us to have contact with them, what they have left behind provides a great challenge for us. This book is an invitation to take up that challenge.

The first three chapters contain discussions of basic problems that set the stage for the archaeology discussed in the remainder of the book. With chapter 4, then, our journey through the ages begins.

1

Unearthing the Leftovers of Ancient Peoples

Let us begin by asking what it is that archaeologists are up to when they pick through the rubbish of ancient cultures. That is a question on people's minds when they visit Native American sites in the southwestern United States, or the ruins of a Celtic settlement in England, or a Roman city in Germany. Modern visitors to Israel and Jordan have the same curiosity when they see an excavation in progress while visiting these countries. And even if many people have never traveled to that part of the world, most likely they will have been captivated at some point by news of a revolutionary discovery made in a cave or a tomb, or among the ruins of an ancient city.

Archaeology in the Near Eastern lands is a subject in which the public has become increasingly interested. Excellent museums in large cities and on university campuses throughout the world have provided opportunities for people to learn about the old cultures of this important region. Many college and university students from the United States, Great Britain, and Europe have enriched their college years by volunteering to help on a summer excavation, and an increasing number of working adults or retired people have set aside time to participate in a "dig." We will probably be surprised to find out, though, that even though archaeology deals with age-old things that have been covered over by soil and debris for centuries, it has only been in recent times that methods have been developed for retrieving this invaluable information. Archaeology is a very young field of investigation, but in its brief existence it has transformed our thinking about people and cultures in most parts of the world. So young is it that it is possible to say that the birth of modern Palestinian archaeology occurred little more than 100 years ago.

Three terms that are important for Palestinian archaeologists are *stratigraphy*, *typology*, and *balks*. *Stratigraphy* refers to the way soils get laid down on top one another, either through human activity or through natural process. *Typology* is the study of common shapes and forms in objects such as pottery, tools, or weapons. It is a key to understanding cultural objects at a site and helps to show relations between sites with similar objects. The term *balks* refers to vertical walls of soil that are left standing during excavation, so that the archaeologist can observe the stratigraphy in them.

To get an idea of some of the changes that have occurred in Palestinian archaeology, imagine what it was like to be on a dig in about 1900. At that time Palestinian archaeology was just beginning to develop some basic methods; therefore, its approaches were understandably quite primitive by modern standards. Early expeditions often lacked a well-thought-out method of excavation and interpretation. Some digs could even be said to have been little more than treasure-hunting expeditions, as workers were instructed to watch out for precious objects, for which they were given special payment. Many excavators had not yet recognized the importance of stratigraphy in digging, and thus long, deep trenches were often cut through the middle of a site, leaving it in a condition that made it difficult for later archaeologists to examine with more refined methods. Usually when a wall appeared in the debris, it was followed to expose the building as a whole, but the abutting soils, which stratified excavation would later prove were crucial for the dating and character of a structure, were also cut away without serious examination.

Fifty years later things had changed. By this time archaeologists had come to recognize how important it was to "locate" their finds in a stratified sequence, and careful attention began to be paid to *where* things were found—in other words, to their context. Digs now used a surveyor to lay out a grid over the site, fixing corner points for "squares" to be excavated. Staff meetings were held in which beginners were introduced to concerns such as stratigraphy, typology, and balks. Detailed attention to soil layers was stressed to those new to the field, because it was the soils that would help to open up the hidden information of the archaeological past. Those participating on a dig would learn how to keep a detailed log book, as well as how to make accurate drawings of features excavated in the squares.

More recently the term *interdisciplinary* has come to define the practice of archaeology in Jordan and Israel. Specialists in a variety of fields, including a good number of the sciences, are now normally members of the staff, along with field archaeologists. Digging deals not only with larger remains of buildings or objects, but also with micro-remains, such as seeds that are separated from soils by sifting or floating them out. Physical anthropologists study human skeletal remains. Computers are brought into the field, and new ways of mapping, high-speed photography, and remote sensing of archaeological sites have been introduced.

Above all, archaeologists now focus on problems they want to solve in their excavations. They are very much aware of why they are working at this site or in this region and not another, and what they hope to solve by working there. And this is interesting, because one of the frequently asked questions of archaeologists is "What are you looking for?" That question, although it may seem very simple, lies behind modern investigation of material remains of ancient cultures.

Of course, while we recognize the strides forward that have been made in the understanding and practice of archaeology today, this does not mean that the work of earlier expeditions has been without value. Archaeologists at any time have to carry on their work according to the technical and theoretical capacities they possess at the time. It is a law of research that scholars in subsequent periods will inevitably discover ways to do things better. Archaeological investigation today has its own successes to enjoy, but it has to be said that its solutions, too, are not final, and future generations will advance our knowledge.

THE NEW ARCHAEOLOGY IN PALESTINE

A phrase that Palestinian archaeologists often use today is *new archaeology*, by which they mean some significant changes that have revolutionized the practice of archaeology. The phrase *new archaeology* comes in part from the archaeology of the New World, and represents one of the important influences of methods and theory that have been developed in the United States, as well as Great Britain. Both of these countries have experienced long histories of research into their own aged cultures. And since in both lands the early native societies were usually nonliterate, researchers have had to develop methods to reconstruct those cultures apart from written information from and about them.

New archaeology of this type differs from that practiced in lands where writing systems existed. In the case of the classical world of Greece and Rome, as well as lands of the Near East, traditional archaeology has concentrated on the excavation of temples, palaces, or libraries where the elites of a society were active. In addition to the possibility that such buildings might produce treasures attracting media attention and public support, it was hoped they might also contain written materials such as tablets or inscriptions. In itself the search for ancient texts was not invalid, but it limited many other possibilities for this kind of investigation. Archaeology undertaken at biblical sites in Israel or Jordan has also sometimes been done by researchers whose primary interest has been to make discoveries helping to explain biblical texts and events.

In the case of the cultures of the New World and Europe, however, where a writing system did not exist, archaeologists have had to reconstruct ancient societies from their nonwritten remains. This has led the newer archaeology to deal with different problems, such as explaining the social structures of societies, as well as exploring the relationship people have had with their environment. The goals include finding out how a society as a whole (not just its political leadership) functioned. Who were the people who lived at a site? What were their houses like? What activities did they carry on in their dwellings? What type of farming did they practice, and what sort of food did they eat? To answer such questions, close attention has also been paid to theory and method which, it is asserted, determine the conception of an archaeological project from beginning to end, including fieldwork and the publications that follow. The search for answers to problems such as these calls for a staff that is truly interdisciplinary. Even for historical and classical archaeologists, who have the advantages of textual remains to go with their finds, the perspectives on society brought by the new archaeology have opened up many new dimensions of inquiry.

It is because of such questions that most Palestinian expeditions now include geologists, paleoethnobotanists, physical anthropologists, zooarchaeologists, and palynologists, in addition to the usual field archaeologists, surveyors, persons skilled in drafting, photographers, and ceramic experts. It is also common practice for expeditions to conduct extensive surveys of the region around a site before excavation begins. Such surveys, done with modern equipment, give a preview of data bearing on the problems the expedition hopes to solve.

WHAT ARCHAEOLOGISTS TODAY ARE LOOKING FOR

To the question about what they hope to find, then, modern archaeologists answer that they are out to provide new ways of viewing the social, economic, cultural, historical, and environmental conditions under which ancient societies lived.

We look first at how people related to their environments. So significant is this subject that one scholar, Karl Butzer, has written a book entitled *Archaeology as Human Ecology,* in which he discusses many of the ways in which archaeological work explores the interaction between humans and their environment.

Studying the effects of the environment is a two-way street. The environment plays a determinative role in the way people settle an area, but people also have an impact on the environment and its resources. If we begin with the way the environment affects people, we are led to look at how various landforms, vegetation, rainfall, animals, trees, and other resources determined people's lifeways. This is where archaeologists are assisted by geologists and other specialists who deal with the environmental realities of the past.

We can think about the term *environment* in a number of ways. First is the *world environment* at the time of a particular culture. Modern earth science has helped us understand the changes our earth has undergone and continues to undergo. These gradual but often extensive shifts, such as in climate or rainfall, are of great relevance when studying ancient societies. Recent investigations in the Negev and the Sinai Peninsula, for example, have shown that during the Upper Paleolithic period, about 40,000 to 20,000 years ago, the entire area was wetter than it is today. Consequently, a good number of occupational sites continue to be discovered dating to this wet phase. That situation has to be contrasted with later conditions in the Negev and the Sinai Peninsula, such as around 2300 B.C.E., when these regions became very arid. Temperature and rainfall greatly influence the general environment, and it is now recognized that the eastern Mediterranean has seen cycles of wetter and drier periods, bearing on the ecology of the region.

We can also think of the environment as the *local* or *regional ecology* affecting settlements at any one time. Archaeologists ask what resources, such as water, soil types, plant life, or trees, were present during the period of settlement. And they attempt to determine the extent of the region on which a people was dependent for subsistence. The parameters of an early hunting and gathering community would be distant from the camp, since such people had to go quite far in search of provisions for survival. A village based on agricultural and horticultural production, on the other hand, would not need to be related to anything more than the lands of the surrounding region. Exchange of goods with other areas would often have some impact on people, but many cases exist where village peoples survived quite well with few or no exports or imports.

A third way of thinking about the environment's impact is its effect upon *human perception*. This angle is important because it introduces the element of human response. While modern archaeological researchers analyze the environment of a given area using scientific methods, most likely ancient people did not assess their surroundings in this manner. Attention to perception has great value in that it has opened up research into the ways the ancients perceived the sites where they settled, or possible reasons why they may have abandoned a region.

For archaeologists, the dimension of environmental investigation is of special importance. This type of study has a bearing on problems such as why a formerly nonsedentary people may have decided to settle down at a site, or what led people to build cities with walls about them. An interesting biblical question concerns what conditions led the Israelite tribes to locate them-

Figure 1.1. The geologist studying the soils at Bab edh-Dhra.

selves at formerly unsettled hill country sites during the first years of their occupation.

Not only did the environmental possibilities affect human beings but people also brought about radical changes to the environment by means of their settlements and the exploitation of natural resources necessary to support them. Understandably, this is the area in which the excavation part of archaeology has the most to contribute. When a people decides to settle an area, they will have a sizable impact upon the natural setting of that area. Trees will be cut down to make room for buildings, to provide material for buildings, or to ready areas for cultivation. Stones will be collected for construction purposes. Natural water supplies will be diverted or collected in new ways to supply water for cultivation, or for drinking and cooking needs. Roads may be constructed. And a variety of smaller items will be sought out, such as clays for making pottery, stones for mortars, chert for flint tools, and small stones for jewelry.

An example of the consequences of the exploitation of the natural environment has been recognized by those who have studied the Early Bronze Age (see chapter 6). During the heyday of this period, extensive tree cutting took place, as documented by excavations at Jericho and Bab edh-Dhra. The Early Bronze Age city builders felled trees for use in building their often large structures. Extensive cutting apparently lowered the water table at Jericho, while at Bab edh-Dhra two large towers flanking an entry to the city were built with a combination of stone, brick, and a large number of timber beams spliced between layers of small stone and brick.

Such data have led interdisciplinary teams at both sites to conclude that the landscape of the regions around Jericho and Bab edh-Dhra had many more trees in antiquity than today. At present, Jericho is still an impressive oasis site with many palm trees, but the hills around the area are seriously denuded. The same is true at Bab edh-Dhra, where prior to the Early Bronze Age many more trees must have stood on the hills and in the valleys. Later peoples also left their mark on these two regions, but the activities of the Early Bronze Age peoples changed the environment for all time to come.

Another example of environmental impact was the practice of terracing the steep slopes of the hill country so that they could be used for agriculture. This technique allowed cultivation to be practiced on hilly areas and not only in plains or valleys. Such an innovation left its mark on the hill country, making possible a denser population in this entire area and opening new frontiers for settlement. Archaeological survey has not fully clarified when such terracing activities were introduced, but they probably preceded the entry of the Israelites into these hilly regions. On the other hand, it seems that certain of the Israelite groups made special use of this method, which provided an impetus to settlement in the hill country. In contrast to tree felling, terracing had the positive effect of helping protect the slopes from erosion. Nonetheless, when the terrace walls were not maintained, erosion could get out of hand and top soils could move into the valleys or streams.

To sum up, today's modern excavations begin their work by defining the environmental problems to which they wish to give attention. Surveying conducted prior to excavation suggests some of the problems that will be met, but the picture becomes more complex as each excavation season proceeds. The search for such information calls for interdisciplinary collaboration. Those supervising the excavations must consult regularly with the geologist and other staff members in order to ascertain the importance of ecological data coming from the areas under excavation.

RECONSTRUCTING ANCIENT SOCIETIES

A further important aspect of modern investigation of ancient remains is what is sometimes referred to as *social archaeology,* a type of archaeology that tries to reconstruct how ancient people organized their common lives. This is a fruitful area of investigation simply because the social organization of ancient peoples is something archaeological information can sometimes cast light upon.

There is much that archaeology can never determine. It cannot really know the minds and emotions of people in antiquity. Even

How did ancient people look at the prospects for settling at a site, and what were the resources available to them when they settled there? Once they did begin to build their village or city, how did they arrange its construction? Archaeology in Palestine today is devoted to gathering data that will help to reconstruct as much about the ancient society as the material remains will allow. Its aim is to learn about life as it was lived by the people of these past societies. This kind of study not only illuminates the dynamics of their social organization, but it also allows modern people to identify with problems that the ancients faced, and may or may not have solved successfully.

as far as written documents of the past are concerned, only a small number of ancient texts give us insights into the feelings of those who wrote them. The same is the case with the cultural items unearthed. We do not know how people felt when they buried their dead. We can excavate their tombs and note the care with which they interred the deceased, but we have no definite clues about their emotional life. We do not know whether they wept, danced, prayed, or did some other religious activity when they placed burials in a tomb. We do not know how people felt about the things they built. We have no access to the potter's feelings about pottery being made. In most cases we can only infer feelings from the way we might react today.

Because of the limitations of what archaeological remains can tell us of the emotive life of ancient people, older archaeology tended to focus on architecture, on describing walls and buildings. But this can be a rather drab objective, and many reports of Palestinian expeditions are tedious to read since they focus on details of walls found in one excavated area or another. While such information is indispensable for reconstruction, reports of this sort have lacked what the newer archaeology calls "an attention to socially significant data." In other words, while archaeology cannot bring to light much in the way of information dealing with the individual, it can illuminate some things about the corporate and social lives of people.

Human beings act not simply on an individual basis, but as part of a social group. Some of the larger social patterns people share, such as nomadism, village life, or urban settlement, are discussed in different chapters below. Here we call attention to smaller units of socially conditioned human behavior. During excavation, evidence frequently comes to light showing how people arranged their dwellings. Within the houses themselves data may indicate how areas were used—whether for food preparation, storage, or for keeping animals. Some buildings undoubtedly had special purposes, such as for pottery-making or flint-knapping. Room and house sizes can also indicate average numbers of people in a family, or the status of the family itself.

Of particular value in studying social patterns is the evidence from burial grounds. Although burial evidence has to be used with caution since it deals with a very special situation in human experience, a person's role in a society might be evident from the type of treatment accorded her or him in death. Sites containing burial along with settlement evidence have special importance for the discussions about social archaeology.

When the findings of social archaeology are introduced into the discussions of the more traditional historical archaeology, new insights into the study of ancient societies emerge. The social emphasis in archaeology today is proving to be a fruitful way to establish connections between Palestinian archaeology on the one hand, and study of the Bible on the other. The socially significant data coming from the investigation of Christian, Jewish, and Islamic sites is also opening up exciting perspectives on these early communities, as will be seen in later chapters.

TECHNOLOGY AND AGRICULTURE

Yet a further subject in which new archaeology has spurred an interest is the social and environmental impact of technology. Older archaeological expeditions were aware of the importance of metals, such as copper or iron, for revolutions in agriculture or the military. These excavations recorded the metals and drew and photographed them; staff members wrote articles about them. What is different in the newer archaeology is that the study of technology is seen as one of the principal determinants in a society's development. That is, technology is viewed as an element in the way a society relates to the resources of its environment.

One important way of understanding the role of technology in a society is through a systems approach to the cultural remains. Systems theory offers a method for thinking about problems of social and economic change. The guiding idea is that change in one aspect of culture has a ripple effect on other aspects. A systems approach assumes that societies are pliable enough to be stimulated by and to experience change. This does not mean that there will not be pockets of resistance to change, but such resistance is usually unsuccessful, at least in the long run. Systems archaeologists view this process much like a chess game–if one piece is moved, the locations of the other pieces are affected.

Therefore, when a technological innovation is introduced, a society experiences change in other areas as well. Several examples will help to visualize this. The invention of pottery took place in the second part of the Neolithic period (called Pottery Neolithic A and B at Jericho). It is difficult to overestimate the importance that the introduction of pottery had for the people of the Neolithic period. With pottery it became possible to carry on a variety of culturally related activities that could not have been done before. Pottery had an impact on the way food was prepared and served. In the course of time, as new types of serving dishes were introduced, the ways families gathered for eating changed. Storage containers also opened new possibilities for preserving food supplies. The invention of pottery provided certain members of the society with the opportunity to become specialists in this craft. Thus, the division between Pre-Pottery Neolithic and Pottery Neolithic is of much greater importance than simply documenting that pottery began at this time. The division points to a change that affected many other aspects not only of that society but also of those that would follow.

Another example is the introduction of iron. As metals go, the durability of iron allowed a variety of new implement forms to be developed. With iron it became possible to advance beyond the common harvesting tools of flint and chert to create a new assemblage of nonlithic tools for farming. The efficiency of the metal implements resulted in larger and better harvests, and this in turn had an impact upon the standard of living, as well as on the number of people who could reside in a particular region.

Yet a further illustration of a technological change more subtle and thus more difficult to trace was the domestication of certain plant types. From the evidence of paleobotanical remains from excavations, it seems that the grape was domesticated sometime during the third millennium B.C.E., that is, during the Early Bronze Age. Quite likely during this same period other horticultural items, such as the olive, became more intensively cultivated, if not domesticated, for the first time. The cultivation of grapes led to the production of wine, so that ancient Palestine was to become famous for its viticulture during the following centuries. Wine from this region was in demand and became one of the exported items affecting the economy. Certain pottery

Figure 1.2. Excavators at Numeira uncover stone-lined storage pits.

vessels were also created for storing and shipping wine as well as olive oil.

Technological change, whether in metallurgy or agriculture, thus has a pervasive effect upon societies. The point is not to advance technological determinism in explaining features of a society. Rather, it shows how a shift in the socioeconomic fabric at one point has a vibrating effect on other aspects of the system. As it is practiced presently, Palestinian archaeology finds itself searching for data along the lines of systemic change, an approach that is to a large extent also a contribution from more recent archaeology.

TRADE AND EXCHANGE OF GOODS

Finally, new research has challenged archaeologists to find better ways to understand the dynamics of trade. Traded items have always been recognized in the finds of excavations. From a social perspective trade mechanisms are seen in the larger framework of a society's organization of resources and the way it made these available to other areas of the country or region. Such study has been aided greatly by the development of scientific analytical methods for examining artifacts. These analyses have often been able to show how items at one site were received from another site, frequently over quite a distance.

The term *trade* has sometimes been used rather loosely, and therefore it must be carefully defined if it is to be useful for archaeological understanding. An object found in one area but originating in another region does not necessarily mean that a trade network between the two regions was in effect. Objects can move from one area to another for any of a number of different reasons. An individual, family, or tribe could travel from their area to another, carrying some of their home items with them. Their objects might be left in the second region, but their presence would not constitute evidence for trade. Similarly, a visitor to another region might bring a foreign item to the home site, in which case the presence of such an object would suggest private travel rather than trade.

Technically, trade assumes larger social organization. It indicates the exploitation of resources in one area that are made available to consumers in another region. In recent archaeology trade has focused on identifying the production centers of certain goods and establishing the manner in which items fan out to appear in secondary areas. Transport could be by overland routes or by sea. In the case of overland dissemination of a product, trade routes may be determined by mapping sites where the product has been found. It follows that sites closer to the production center will contain a larger number of the imported goods, while lesser amounts will appear farther from the center. Such studies have recently been applied to certain types of pottery that were either themselves the item traded or contained the traded items, such as wine or olive oil.

A society in a production center will most likely evidence a complex form of organization. Trade activity assumes that specialized groups at the home base were engaged in the acquisition of items and their preparation for export. Entrepreneurs were also involved in making contacts with other areas and setting up arrangements by which items were shipped from one region to another. In a technical sense, trade could also be manifested at much simpler levels. Even mobile pastoralists might have "traded" certain items for others as they moved into different regions. It seems best, however, to reserve the word *trade* for the more intensive organization of complex societies. *Exchange* may be a better term with which to describe the simpler give-and-take of less complex societies.

An interdisciplinary approach to cultural remains adds a positive contribution to the study of trade connections. Expeditions commonly submit various objects to technical analysis following the work in the field. Pottery is examined petrographically, or by neutron activation analysis; these analyses can often help determine where the pottery came from. Precious stones used for jewelry-making are studied in their geologic context; this often yields information about where the stone may have been obtained. Shells can be similarly identified as to whether they came from the Mediterranean or the Red Sea. An entire area of research has also sprung up around the identification of plant remains and the most likely places where they were grown. Foodstuffs, too, were transported from one area to another, constituting trade transaction.

All features discussed in this chapter—environment, social organization, technology, agriculture, and trade—interact with each other and are best viewed as components in a single system. Archaeologists today make use of a more holistic framework in tracing the beginnings, growth, and decline of the different societies during Palestine's long history.

2
The Land and Its Resources

Human settlements are related to their surroundings, which means that in many ways the physical features of the Palestinian landscape are the place to begin in studying the archaeology of the area. In this chapter, therefore, we shall be looking at the mountain ranges, plains, deserts, rivers, and springs that characterize different regions of the country. We shall also survey the more common plants and animals that were exploited by the various peoples of antiquity. Then, in the last part of the chapter, we shall take up a matter with which archaeological expeditions are often concerned—the problem of matching present-day archaeological ruins with places mentioned in ancient documents such as the Bible or inscriptions in Egypt.

But we should first explain the term *Palestine* that will be used in the chapters below. The designation *Palestine* is derived from the ancient name of the Philistines, one of the peoples who began to arrive as new settlers about 1200 B.C.E. (they are dealt with in chapter 8). The Philistines are mentioned in a number of ancient Near Eastern texts, and they are described in the Bible as mostly antagonistic to the early Israelites (1 Samuel 4).

The use of the term *Palestine* to denote this country as a whole did not occur until much later, however. It was the Romans who chose the Latin form, *Palaestina*, to designate the land of Canaan and Israel as part of their eastern empire. And it was consequently this usage by the Romans that imprinted the name Palestine on the region more or less continuously for the next twenty centuries. It is common for archaeologists in Israel and Jordan today to use the designation for the region encompassed by the State of Israel, the West Bank, and the Hashemite Kingdom of Jordan. This is the way we shall be using it in this book.

As we survey this small but very diverse land, it will be convenient to think of the Palestinian landscape according to seven major regions. The first four of these follow a more or less north-south orientation. The fifth and sixth lie mostly east-west. And the seventh is a large region lying to the south.

THE COASTAL PLAIN

On its western side, the country of modern Israel shares with other lands of the eastern Mediterranean an extensive coastal plain. This plain is a two- to ten-mile wide strip of white and reddish sandy flatland, beginning near Haifa, and continuing south of Tel Aviv. Since the shoreline is relatively straight, almost no natural harbors existed, making it necessary to create artificial breakwaters at sites such as Caesarea Maritima and Dor. The part of this coastal area between modern Tel Aviv and Haifa was known in antiquity as the Sharon Plain, immortalized in the words of the biblical Song of Songs: "I am a rose of Sharon, a lily of the valleys" (Song of Sol. 2:1).

Although sandy soils predominate in the coastal plain, a rich alluvium is also found, making the plain an excellent growing area for fruits. At the eastern end of the plain the flatland meets the lower edges of the hill country. Several ancient trunk roads leading from the coastal plain into the hill country entered the latter at this point. Closer to the Mediterranean was also the ancient roadway called "the way of the sea," one of the major routes between the north and south. Although the coastal plain presented difficulties for the establishment of settlements, large cities such as Aphek were well established by the year 2000 B.C.E. During Hellenistic, Roman, Byzantine, Crusader, and Islamic times, the region saw the development of sizable settlements, such as at Caesarea Maritima and Dor. Today several of the largest cities in Israel represent modern examples of coastal urbanism.

THE CENTRAL HILL COUNTRY

East of the coastal plain is a highland area extending from the Judean hills northward to the region of Galilee. This central hill country follows a north-south direction and is dissected by the broad Esdraelon plain (also known as the Plain of Jezreel) on the northeast side of the Mount Carmel range. North of the Esdraelon plain the area is once more elevated, joining with the hills of northern Israel and the mountainous regions of southern Lebanon. In addition to the Esdraelon plain, the hill country also has a number of small valleys, but only a few of these, such as the Shechem plain with its ancient city by the same name, were used for valley settlement during ancient times. In addition to Shechem, some of the Bible's most important cities, such as Shiloh, Samaria, and Jerusalem, were located in the hill country.

As will be seen in several discussions below, it was in the hill country that the Israelites first settled. This was a much less promising region than the valleys and plains with their rich natural resources. The hills were often rocky and soils were difficult to work. Springs were not abundant, so the water supply was an ongoing problem.

In addition, the higher hills of this area promoted isolationism since it was difficult for people in one subregion to maintain contact with occupants in another. Thus people in the Judean hills in the south rarely had contact with inhabitants in Galilee in the north. These conditions were no doubt a contributing factor to the division of the northern and southern Israelite kingdoms (see chapter 10).

THE JORDAN RIFT VALLEY

Undoubtedly the most striking feature of Palestine is the extensive Rift Valley that today divides the West Bank and parts of Israel from the modern Hashemite Kingdom of Jordan east of the river. Tectonic activity before and during the Pleistocene age (*c.* 1,000,000 years ago) resulted in a north-south graben or deep depression (Arabic: *ghor*), bordered by mountain slopes on its east and west sides. The rift is found not only in the area of Palestine itself, but can be followed northward into Turkey. To the south the depression in which the Dead Sea began to take its present form some 20,000 to 25,000 years ago was part of this rift, as were also the Araba and Red seas. The same rift structure continues into the east African continent.

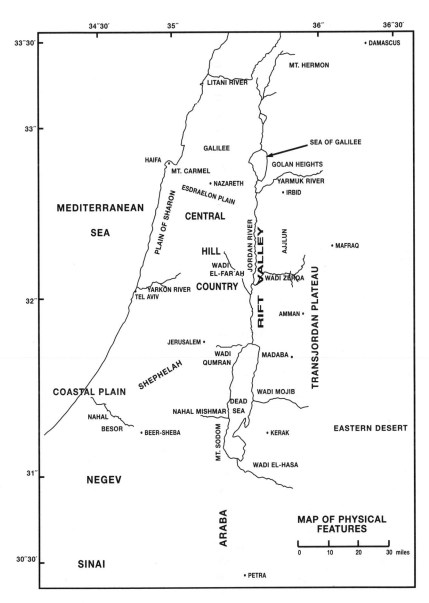

Figure 2.1. Map of the main features of ancient Palestine.

Since more rainfall occurs in the northern latitudes, the environment of the Rift Valley just south of the Sea of Galilee offers better natural resources for settlement. South of the Dead Sea, and particularly in the Araba, the area is extremely arid. Settlement there was more sparse than in the northerly region. One exception to this was the southeastern plain adjacent to the Dead Sea, where archaeological survey and excavations during the past two decades have brought to light cities of the Early Bronze Age and substantial occupation during Roman, Byzantine, Crusader and Islamic times.

THE TRANSJORDAN PLATEAU

East of the Rift Valley in modern Jordan the hills reach high elevations. It was on this highland that the ancient civilizations of Transjordan were situated. The modern capital of Amman is in the heart of this region. North of Amman are hills and valleys comparable to the hill country west of the Jordan River, while northwest of Amman is the rich forest region of Ajjlun. The region east of Amman merges into a vast desert stretching southward into Saudi Arabia. In the Jordan desert occasional oases such as the one at Azraq are found. Along the high tableland just east of the Dead Sea, the landscape is often dissected by spectacular gorges (called *wadis* in Arabic). The Wadi Mojib (biblical: Arnon), for example, presents a breathtaking sight when viewed from its northern rim.

The high Transjordan mountains are found along the east side of the Araba all the way to the Red Sea. In one area a natural red-to-orange Nubian sandstone has been laid bare, and it is in this spectacular environment that the famous Nabataean city of Petra was created (see chapter 12). Southeast of Petra at Ras en-Naqb a drop in elevation occurs, leading into the ruggedly beautiful area called the Hisma. In this large area is located the Wadi Rum, famous for its splendid views.

THE PLAIN OF ESDRAELON

The Esdraelon plain, the eastern part of which was known in biblical times as the Valley of Jezreel, is the largest inland plain in the entire region. Beginning on the northern flanks of Mount Carmel, the plain stretches southeastward to the Jordan valley.

The Esdraelon plain is one of the most fertile areas west of the Jordan River. Wheat, melons, and vegetable products have been grown in this area since antiquity. Given its favorable resources and steadier annual rainfall, the area was the location of some of the large cities of Canaan and Israel, such as Megiddo, Taanach, Yoqneam, and Ibleam. The ruins near modern Afula also indicate a settlement of substantial size. A good number of important historical events, including military encounters, occurred in this plain.

THE LOWLANDS

Southwest of Jerusalem the hilly country becomes lower in elevation. Beginning at about Beth Shemesh and continuing farther west to the modern city of Gath, this lowland area was called the Shephelah during biblical times. The term *shephelah* comes from a Hebrew word meaning "to be low." In the Shephelah were such ancient cities as Yarmuth, Lachish, Beth Shemesh, Gezer, and Ekron, the latter two sites also bordering on the coastal plain. The area of the Shephelah is wider from east to west than from north to south. It also receives enough rain to make it a fertile region for farming. Not posing as many problems as did the hill country for cultivation, the region witnessed the emergence of large settlements. Historically, the cities of this area also figure prominently in recorded events.

The Shephelah also contained a good tree cover in antiquity. Almonds, olives, and grapes were grown here. Cattle were also raised in this region, as they are today.

THE NEGEV

The term *Negev* means "southland." This region is a predominantly arid one that begins south of the Shephelah and extends to the northern part of the Sinai Peninsula. To the west the Negev joins with the southwestern coastal area along the Mediterranean, while to the east it ends at the edges of the hills that plunge to the Dead Sea.

The most important city of the Negev in antiquity was Beersheba, located, as its Hebrew name "Seven Wells" implies, alongside a productive water source. Other significant cities were established over time from the third millennium B.C.E. down to

Byzantine time. Despite the fact that the Negev receives much less rainfall than the hill country, peoples of the past often demonstrated their ingenuity in catching what water was available. This was primarily runoff from winter rains, but the development of catchment systems made possible an impressive agricultural industry in this desertic region. Since the Negev borders on the Sinai, the sites are often important for the information they offer regarding relations between Palestine and Egypt during different historical periods.

CLIMATE AND RAINFALL

Palestine's climate is determined by the fact that it lies between the Mediterranean Sea on the west, the Arabian desert on the east and south, and the mountains of Asia to the north. Situated between 30° and 33° latitude, Palestine is in a semitropical zone. This means that it has mainly two seasons of the year, winter and summer. Only in a few wooded areas of the country where deciduous trees are found can anything resembling colorful fall foliage be found. During a short spring season beginning in February many open fields display a panorama of wild flowers. Between April and October the entire area becomes hot and dry, with temperatures reaching 115°F in unusually hot periods, while from November through March intermittent rains and cool or even cold days are normal. Snow is rare, but snowfalls occur occasionally in the more mountainous regions, such as around Jerusalem or in the Jordan mountains north and south of Amman.

A great variety of rainfall amounts exists in the different regions of this relatively small area of the eastern Mediterranean, a fact that has had an impact on agricultural development in the differing areas. Rainfall originates usually from the Mediterranean Sea, although showers may develop from both easterly and southerly directions. The largest amount of rainfall is dropped on the mountainous central and northern parts of the country. As the clouds move across from the Mediterranean, they deposit some precipitation on the coastal plain, saving much of it for the mountains west of the Jordan River, then sometimes skipping over the Rift Valley to deposit more rain on the central and northern Transjordan mountains.

In both Israel and Jordan the amount of rainfall even in the mountain ranges decreases substantially south of Jerusalem and Amman, so that the southern areas of both countries are arid. In Israel the Negev receives only occasional outbursts of rain, and in some years almost none, while the same is the case in the increasingly arid areas south of Ma'an in Jordan. This means that settlements in the southerly regions were dependent on irrigation agriculture, in contrast to hill country settlements where runoff or cistern-stored rainwater provided a source for domestic and agricultural use.

A special case is the southern region of the Rift Valley, known as the Dead Sea and its environs. This region is an unusual one, since it not only occupies an area with an extremely limited rainfall per year (the average is fifty millimeters), but also contains several perennial springs. The exploitation of these spring waters feeding into the Dead Sea encouraged thriving settlements in this harsh environment during a number of archaeological periods.

WATER CARRIERS

Ancient settlements were often located near prominent features of the landscape. Since Arabic or Hebrew terms are often used for these natural features, it will be useful to know the meaning of some of the main terms.

Palestine has no large rivers to compare with major rivers of the world. The Jordan River is well known because of its importance in the Bible, but it is a small stream in comparison to larger rivers in other areas of the world. The Jordan River system forms as a result of runoff from the Lebanon mountains. These waters gather first in the Sea of Galilee before the river itself leaves the sea at the latter's south end. Flowing southward through the Jordan valley, the river picks up additional water from the tributary Wadis Yarmuk and Zerqa that enter from the east. As the crow flies, the Jordan River covers an area of about sixty-five miles between the Sea of Galilee and the Dead Sea, but its snake-like course means that it covers a much greater distance. At some time in antiquity the water covered the entire Jordan valley that near Jericho is over two miles wide. Today, however, the river is less than 100 feet wide.

One other stream that may be referred to as a river is the Yarkon, whose mouth occurs at the Mediterranean shore just north of Tel Aviv. This stream, too, is small by comparison with rivers in other areas of the world, but it is fed by a perennial spring with a copious supply of water located at the site of ancient Aphek. The remainder of streams are more erratic, and flow through gorges during the rainy winter months, their streams diminishing to a trickle during the hot summer. Such streams are known in Arabic by the term *wadi*, and in Hebrew *nahal*. There are a good number of these streams on both sides of the Jordan valley. On the east side of the river and the Dead Sea in Jordan are major wadis such as the Wadi Zerqa (Nahal Yabbok), the Wadi Mojib (Nahal Arnon), and the Wadi el-Hasa (Nahal Zered). In Israel are the Nahal Besor in the Negev, the Wadi Qneieh near Tel Aviv, and the Wadi el-Far'ah that opens up into the Jordan valley. Near the site of the discovery of the Dead Sea scrolls is also the Wadi Qumran.

In addition to wadis, perennial springs are a treasured water source. Often these springs create oases, and thus many of the settlements of antiquity were founded around them. The Hebrew and Arabic words for springs are similar, *'en* in Hebrew, *'ayn* in Arabic. Different from springs are manmade cisterns or wells. Arabic uses the word *bir* and Hebrew *be'er* for this feature. Cisterns were designed to catch rainwater. A cylindrical shaft lined with stones was constructed through the softer soil above bedrock. The shaft was then joined with the bell of the cistern cut deep into the bedrock, and it was here that the water was collected. Many place names in Palestine have incorporated the words for *spring* or *cistern* into them, such as 'En-Gedi in Hebrew or 'Ayn Jiddi in Arabic, and Bir-seba in Arabic and Beer-sheba in Hebrew.

LANDFORMS

Three major landforms are found in the country: mountains (or hills), plains, and deserts. Mountains are referred to in Arabic by the term *jebel*. An example is the hilly range on the southwest side of the Dead Sea, called in Arabic Jebel Usdum from the tradition that ancient Sodom was located nearby. Hebrew uses two words for hills: *har*, a hilly, sometimes mountainous region, and *giv'ah*, commonly used for a hill. Plains are referred to by similar terms in the two languages—*'emeq* in Hebrew and *'amuq* in Arabic. Thus the Plain of Jezreel is called in the Hebrew Bible the 'Emeq Jezreel.

Since a large part of the region of Palestine consists of desert or wilderness, individual names were often attributed to subareas of wastelands of this type. Thus the region between Jerusalem and the Dead Sea was known as the Judean Desert. Hebrew uses the term *midhbar* for the desert areas. Parts of the Jordan tableland east of the Dead Sea were viewed as wilderness, and several regions in the Sinai Peninsula were referred to in the same fashion, such as the Wilderness of Sin or the Wilderness of Paran. In these wildernesses can be found evidence of settlement, but obviously, with very few exceptions such as Beer-sheba in the Negev, large cities were not built here.

PLANTLIFE AND TREES

Palestine's climate and its varying elevations and rainfall impose limitations on the type of vegetation found in different parts of the country. A natural and widely present tree in the hilly country is the olive tree *(Olea europaea)*, that grew extensively in antiquity as it does today. Alongside it is the almond *(Amygdalus communis)* that was also a native tree in antiquity. Groves of both olives and almonds are found on many farms in the hill country today. The same region was also known for grapes *(Vitis vinifera)*, and vineyards thrived in the rich brown and red *terra rossa* soils along the hillsides. Also found in the hill country are local oak trees *(Quercus calliprinos)*, terebinths *(Pistacia Palaestina)*, and

In the Bible, trees often marked special locations where an important event occurred. In Gen. 12:6 Abraham stopped at an oak tree in the city of Shechem, after a long journey from Haran. The prophet Jeremiah (Jer. 1:11) was observing an almond tree branch when the word of the Lord came to him. Many of Palestine's assortment of trees are mentioned in the Bible.

junipers *(Juniperus phoenica)*. Terracing increased productivity of the fruit-bearing trees.

In the lower areas of the Jordan valley and the coastal plain the climate and soils are different, so that trees that grow here and foodstuffs that are produced here were very different from those found in the hilly areas. In the Jordan valley, and especially in the plains along the Dead Sea and the Araba, was the prominent acacia tree *(Acacia)* that can accommodate itself to the most desert-like conditions. Also at home in this dry climate was the Christ's-thorn tree *(Zizyphus spina-christi)*. The date palm *(Phoenix dactylifera)* is found in groves along the Mediterranean coast, while the prime growing area for date palms is in the Jordan valley and along the Dead Sea plains. Only the latter tree produced an edible fruit in the arid Dead Sea region.

Although the coastal plain today is known for its cultivation of cotton and citrus fruits, evidence from archaeology suggests that it was mostly grain that was produced here in antiquity. This included several earlier types of wheat such as emmer wheat

Figure 2.2. An acacia tree in the Dead Sea valley.

(*Triticum dicoccum*) and einkorn (*Triticum monococcum*), as well as barley (*Hordeum vulgare*), the latter having grown wild in such places as along the slopes of Mount Carmel. Grapes were also cultivated along the coastal plain, and one of the cities that became famous for its export of wine was the coastal city of Gaza. During the Byzantine period in particular, Gaza wine was sought after by connoisseurs in various parts of the Mediterranean world. Other foodstuffs that grew naturally in the region, and that became cultivated products, were chickpeas (*Cicer arietinum*) and lentils (*Lens esculenta*). The fig tree (*Ficus carica*) was also a staple fruit.

ANIMALS

The popular sheep (*Ovis aries*) and goat (*Capra hircus*) have for millennia been important in the Palestinian cultures. These animals were domesticated well before 7000 B.C.E., and became part of the staple meat diet. Goat milk was used in the production of yogurt (Arabic: *lebn*). Every excavation in Palestine, dealing with any period from 7000 B.C.E. onward, recovers numerous sheep and goat bones. The pastoralist sheepherder was visible everywhere. The cow (*Bos primigenius*) was also an animal of importance for milk and sometimes for meat, while the gazelle (*Gazella dorcasor*) was often hunted and eaten.

For transportation most people depended on the gray-coated donkey (*Equus asinus*). This beast of burden transported water, sacks of grain, or other edibles to the living areas. The donkey was also used to ride from village to village, or was loaded up if people moved from one place to another. As for the camel, the date when this animal first began to be used for transportation has been debated. A common view followed by many is that the camel was introduced around the twelfth century B.C.E. The evidence on which such a date is based is from camel bones found at excavated sites, where it might be assumed that these animals may have been kept for working or transportation purposes.

Wild animals were also present, such as leopards (*Panthera pardus*), lions (*Panthera leopersica*), and hyenas (*Hyaena hyaena*). With the exception of the lion, some of these may still be seen in remote areas of the land today, although much of the wildlife has been killed off. Among the reptiles, the most deadly was the viper *(Echis coloratus)*, still found in the rocky areas of the country today. In the bird class were many species, prominent among which were sparrows and pigeons. Related to the latter was the turtledove *(Streptopelia turtur)*, a fowl noted for its low, murmuring sound.

GEOGRAPHERS AND PALESTINIAN SITES

Because of its importance to the three religions of Judaism, Christianity, and Islam, Palestine was often visited by pilgrims, scholars of religion, and others. The records these early visitors sometimes left behind have special importance, since they give information about the land in antiquity, well before the extensive changes caused by modern urbanization, land cultivation, and industrialization.

One of the earliest writers to record sites in Palestine was the Christian historian and bishop, Eusebius, whose home was in Caesarea along the Mediterranean. In one of his writings, the *Onomasticon*, Eusebius attempted to establish the locations of sites known in the Bible and in early Christian history. Eusebius lived between 260 and 339 c.e., and this particular work, as a number of his other writings, is still today a key source for the study of Palestine as it was known at his time.

So also is the record left by a Christian nun from either Gaul or Spain, who traveled to Palestine and other regions of the Middle East between 381 and 384 c.e. Her name is most likely to be spelled *Egeria*, and she left behind an important diary of her travels. Egeria visited many regions of the country, spent a considerable time in Jerusalem, and was particularly interested in recording goings-on among the Christians in the land at this time. At a later time Muslim pilgrims and travelers also recorded their impressions, which today are of great historical value. One of these was the Arab geographer, Muqaddasi, whose famous work on the geography of Palestine was written about 985 c.e.

During the nineteenth century, explorers from the European countries, Great Britain, and the United States made trips to Palestine to investigate its relatively unknown regions. These travelers recorded information about ruins, the habits of the people living in the land at the time of their visits, and the environment. Their records sometimes included geographic and geological information. Among these travelers were the British explorers Charles Irby and James Mangles, the German Ulrich Seetzen, and the American Edward Robinson. Robinson organized his explorations on a scientific basis, and his work, entitled *Biblical Researches in Palestine,* is still one of the most significant sources for the study of the land and its ancient sites. Later in the third decade of the twentieth century Nelson Glueck carried out a similar type of exploration in the region of modern Jordan.

Today a large number of atlases and geographies of Palestine are available for the study of the land. All of these are indebted to the first modern work of this type, the atlas and geographical study of George Adam Smith, entitled *Historical Geography of Palestine,* published in 1896.

IDENTIFYING ARCHAEOLOGICAL SITES

Basic to the archaeological study of sites in Palestine is their identification. An archaeologist usually begins work with two kinds of information. On the one hand he or she has knowledge of a ruin or tell that has come from preliminary survey or excavation. But also important are references to ancient locations in the Bible, or in documents from Egypt, Syria, or Mesopotamia. The problem then becomes that of identifying places known by name in written documents with archaeological ruins. Any archaeologist working at a site having a connection with place names known in written texts faces this problem. Although this is a complex matter, several of the following issues are involved.

Of special importance is that many ruins or tells of Palestine have names by which local inhabitants call them today. Sometimes these names may not be very old, referring simply to a feature such as a spring near the site. The tell that archaeologists have identified with ancient Megiddo, for example, was called by local people Tell el-Mutesellim. This name, which seems to come from a word suggesting a place of safety, indicates what Arab villagers thought about this tell, but it gives no clue about its ancient name. On the other hand, another mound near Megiddo has the modern name Tell Ta'annek, and it can very quickly be seen that this modern local name has apparently preserved the ancient name of Taanach, found in the Bible and Egyptian texts.

Simply put, there are two kinds of sites so far as identification is concerned: those whose modern names still carry a clear or perhaps distant indication of what their name was in antiquity, and those whose ancient names have been lost from the site. Jerusalem is the classic example of the first type, since it has not lost its name at any time during the past 3,000 years or more. Those whose names have been forgotten obviously present a greater challenge.

But one more problem complicates putting ancient names together with modern names. Sometimes an ancient name may have wandered from its original site. This would have happened when people in times past moved to a new location, carrying the old name with them. This means that the ancient name may be present in the region, but not at the original site of antiquity. Such seems to have been the case with Tell Hesban in Jordan. This site has been thoroughly excavated, but the data found did not easily match up with the description of ancient Heshbon found in the Bible. Although the problem of identifying this site is still not solved, it may be that the name Hesban was transferred to the tell by this name at a later time.

Occasionally it happens that an ancient name of a site occurs on an inscription found at the site itself. A researcher who makes such a discovery is fortunate, since this provides virtually incontrovertible proof for what the site was called in antiquity. The best example from Palestine is a group of inscribed "boundary stones" found at Gezer containing the name of the site. Another example was a group of inscriptions written on broken pieces of pottery called *ostraca*, found at what has been identified as ancient Lachish. One ostracon contained the phrase "we are watching for the signals of Lachish, for we cannot see Azekah." It seems likely that these letters originated from another location, and that they were sent to the site named Lachish in the texts. And thus that would make it a strong likelihood that the site where these ostraca were found was actually Lachish. Incidentally, the modern Arabic name was Tell ed-Duweir, which provides no clue to the ancient name.

Such strokes of good fortune as the discovery of the name of a site on inscriptions found at the site are few and far between. Most efforts at site identification are consequently based on circumstantial evidence. That means an archaeologist has to weigh the evidence as to whether a site's ruins date to the right time to be connected with a known ancient site, and also whether the site's location is compelling enough to propose an identification. Written texts, such as the Bible, or ancient documents found in Egypt or Mesopotamia often indicate the general area where a town or city ought to be located. If such clues are studied in relation to a site under investigation, they may suggest that a particular site could be a good candidate for a place named in written documents. Similarly, since a document in which a place name occurs can often be dated rather closely, there should be material evidence at the archaeological site dating to the same period as reflected in the written material. Because changing pottery forms and decorations can now be closely dated for most periods, it can easily be determined whether a site has evidence for a particular period or not.

Many of the identifications of ancient sites rest on inferences of this type. Biblical Shechem is a good example. The Bible indicates that Shechem was located in the heart of the central hill country of ancient Palestine. It also suggests that it was a major religious site for both Canaanites and Israelites. Excavations at Tell Balata near modern Nablus have shown that this tell most likely contains the ruins of ancient Shechem, despite the fact that no inscriptional evidence to support an identification came from the site. Nor did the modern name, Tell Balata, help for the identification.

It was the circumstantial evidence that made this tell the most convincing candidate for ancient Shechem. Tell Balata sits in the pass between the two mountains, Ebal and Gerizim, a fact that fits well with the biblical description of Shechem's location. And since the excavations proved that the tell was occupied during the Late Bronze and early Iron ages, the dating of the site suits the biblical accounts as well. The exposure by the excavators of a large temple complex also showed the special religious character of this site, something indicated by texts within and outside the Bible.

This kind of discussion about Shechem's location at Tell Balata shows how important the problem of site identification can be. According to the Bible (Judges 9), Shechem was one of the most important cities in the history of the early Israelites. To know its location, and to have fresh evidence from excavation, offers valuable new information. Shechem is only one example. Many other archaeological sites are potential candidates for being identified with places known in written accounts.

3
Finding How Old Things Are

Everything discovered by archaeologists must be dated if it is to have value for reconstructing ancient societies. We have seen that one of the positive contributions of the new archaeology has been that it has moved archaeological investigation beyond a one-sided concern with chronology. It is still true, however, that if cultural remains are not correctly dated, they will lack the context in time that gives them their true significance. Thus, all archaeological work in any part of the world is necessarily concerned with time and dating schemes, and great efforts have been made to develop the best mechanisms to determine the times to which cultural remains are related. The question often asked, "How old is it?," is a basic one.

Establishing a chronology, however, is one of the more difficult problems facing investigators of ancient Palestine because comparatively few written records produced earlier than 1000 B.C.E. have been found. The explanation for this is unclear. Either people in ancient Palestine wrote very little in earlier years or, as is more likely, the writing may have been on perishable material that has not survived. Even the Bible, as will be seen, has little that can be dated before the tenth century B.C.E. For later periods, on the other hand, the picture is much more encouraging. Ruins of Hellenistic or Roman date can often be directly connected with written information. A great deal of documented evidence exists, for example, about Caesarea Maritima on the Mediterranean coast in Israel, and buildings illuminated now by historical texts have been found by excavators at this site. Similarly, Jerusalem is a city about which much early written description existed.

THE BIBLE AND CHRONOLOGY

What does the Bible contribute to chronology problems? The New Testament sometimes gives information that can be correlated with events of the first century c.e. known from other texts. Occasionally it even contains dates known from contemporary historical sources outside the Bible. Such is the reference to the fifteenth year of Tiberius in Luke 3:1, which can be converted to an absolute date of 29 c.e. The New Testament also sometimes records information helpful for interpreting archaeological remains, such as its descriptions of features of the Roman city of Jerusalem, known from extensive excavations done in the temple area and other parts of the city.

The Hebrew Bible, on the other hand, presents us with difficulties, especially in its earlier sections. One event that can be securely dated is the attack against the city of Jerusalem carried out in the nineteenth year of Nebuchadnezzar, that is, in 586 b.c.e. The Bible's description of this event can be compared with a good amount of material outside the Bible dealing with the same event. Not only do we have a group of Babylonian texts that describe this invasion in detail, recent excavations in Jerusalem have also produced an abundance of data related to this destruction (see chapter 10).

Going back earlier, some archaeological remains can also be plausibly related to the period of the kings of Judah and Israel, and even to the times of David and Solomon. But before the time of David, whose reign began about 1000 b.c.e., the possibilities for connections become more obscure. For example, there is the difficult problem of when and how the Israelites entered the land of Canaan. Not only is the Bible's own dating of these events unclear, but the archaeological picture is also complex. An even more disputed issue is whether archaeology has any evidence that can be related to the stories of the ancestors of the people of Israel, as these are recorded in Genesis 12–50. Both of these problems are discussed in other chapters below.

It is important to be aware of these complications in relation to biblical dates and chronology. It is also important to know that most of the dates used in Palestinian archaeology are relative, which means they are simply approximate dates. On the other hand, the relative chronologies that have been worked out are reasonably well grounded, even for the earliest periods. That we are not walking on thin ice in the case of chronology, however, is due to the great amount of attention given to relative dating, especially that dealing with ancient pottery.

As a result of important developments in the sciences, archaeology today has a number of means by which reasonably good dates for artifact groups can be obtained. Some of these are rather sophisticated approaches to the material, and it will be useful to look at several of them.

DATING WITH POTTERY

Pottery has played a particularly important role in the development of the chronological schemes used in Palestinian archaeology. Because clay is such a pliable material, it is theoretically possible to produce a great variety of forms with it. Thus the changes in style and construction have been a key to the chronological importance of pottery-making. Every archaeological site from the Pottery Neolithic period to modern times is characterized by broken pieces of pottery, called sherds, strewn around the site. Excavators collect these pottery fragments and use them to construct a dating scheme.

With the discovery of pottery-making, vessels were produced to serve a variety of purposes. Some types were developed for storage, and others for food preparation or food serving. Still other vessels seem to have had no greater purpose than to emphasize the wealth of those who used them. Some pottery was also produced for special use in religious activities. While in the newer archaeology it has become important to understand the

Pottery-making was one of the extraordinary achievements of early human beings. From the time it began to be made it influenced daily life in almost all areas. Pottery offered new ways of preparing and serving food and thus affected eating habits. It fostered more convenient ways of storage, and thus also contributed to better sanitation and health. It played no small role in the trading activities of peoples. And it stimulated the artistic imaginations of potters, who created special forms for luxury or for ceremonial usages.

social significance of pottery at a site, we are concerned here with its specific importance for dating.

A significant breakthrough in the development of Palestinian archaeology occurred when it was discovered that changes in pottery shapes could help determine when a site was occupied. In 1890, while excavating at Tell el-Hesi, a British archaeologist named Flinders Petrie pioneered a method called "sequence dating." He had already tested this method in excavations in Egypt, but it was in Palestine that he put his approach to a strict test. Petrie's effort was to separate the stratigraphy of the site of Tell el-Hesi according to levels. At approximately every half meter of debris Petrie assigned a sequence date (abbreviated s.d.), placing the pottery found in a position relative to what was below and above it. Petrie was thus the first Palestinian archaeologist to give this kind of attention to the changing features of pottery in association with vertical stratigraphy.

The problem with Petrie's method of excavation was its arbitrary separation of levels. The stratigraphy of Palestinian tells is never so simple as that approach tended to make it. Layers more often wave up and down. Stratigraphy may be disturbed by building activity. Pits dug at a later time may intrude. And many other anomalies are found when the researcher seeks to determine true stratigraphy. These are problems that have received much clarification since Petrie's time.

At this point in the history of Palestinian archaeology, it can be said that we possess a solid pottery chronology for almost all periods beginning with the Neolithic period. Naturally, gaps and uncertainties still exist, but one of the significant achievements of the archaeological work of the past half century is in the area of pottery chronology.

CARBON-14 DATING

While pottery continues to be one of the most important items for dating the remains of a site, the development of new analytical scientific methods has added an independent basis for chronological conclusions. One of the most significant of these is carbon-14 (C-14) testing of archaeological data.

This effective dating tool is so well established that few expeditions today would neglect using it on selected data. Radiocarbon dating is especially critical for the archaeology of prehistoric periods, since it is frequently the most reliable way of dating very early remains. Its value even for later periods was recognized when C-14 datings of the Dead Sea scrolls helped establish their antiquity. In fact, the mechanism of C-14 dating was developed by Willard F. Libbey of the University of Chicago just about the time the Dead Sea Scrolls were discovered in 1947.

It is not difficult to understand the basics of C-14 dating, although a detailed understanding assumes knowledge of chemistry and physics. Simply put, carbon-14 is a radioactive isotope (related to the nonradioactive isotope C-12) found in all living matter. It is produced when cosmic rays bombard the earth's atmosphere, reacting with nitrogen-14, a process that goes on continuously. The production of C-14 ceases immediately with the death of an organism, following which the amount of C-14 in the organism breaks down at a measurable rate. Scientists have determined the half-life of any amount of C-14 to be reached at 5,730 ±40 years, the figure "40 years" being a standard deviation.

This means that when a living plant or organism dies, the amount of C-14 remaining after 5,730 years will be one-half that found in the organism at the time of death. Thus, after 11,460 years, one-fourth of the C-14 would remain, and so on. These measured amounts of C-14 can then be converted into calendar dates.

Obviously, the older the material being studied, the less the amount of C-14 retained. Consequently, limits exist on how far back this method is useful, about 40,000 or 50,000 years ago being the apparent time of its effectiveness. For Palestinian archaeology this would cover all except the earlier phases of the Palaeolithic, for which other analytic techniques, such as potassium argon or amino acid racemization dating, are available.

When Libbey set forth his conclusions on C-14 dating, he assumed that the atmospheric conditions under which it operated were stable. Subsequently it has been shown that other factors affect C-14 in organic matter, such as changes in the earth's magnetic field and the effects of the sun's activity. The development of tree-ring dating also necessitated a recalibration of C-14 dates. Especially important has been the study of the bristlecone pine *(Pinus aristata)*, which is one of the longest living trees in the mid-upper latitudes. Dates for this pine are now available that go back before 5000 B.C.E., including fossilized examples in Europe. All C-14 studies now are thus adjusted to the tree-ring data, and several proposed calibration tables have been published in the literature on C-14 dating.

Since C-14 is influenced by atmospheric and environmental conditions, field workers use care in extracting material to be submitted for analysis. Two factors especially can contaminate samples. One is the person excavating, who by touching or exposing the sample will likely skew its reliability. Atomic radiation tests following World War II have also left an amount of contamination in the atmosphere. It is thus not uncommon to find that samples from near the surface are contaminated by radioactivity of recent making.

When an expedition prepares its materials for study, a selection is made of the most important samples to be sent to a laboratory for C-14 analysis. With the development of high-efficiency procedures in C-14 testing, it is now possible to attain reliable results with very small amounts of material. Due to the costs of such tests, an expedition will usually send only its best collected samples for testing. Laboratories where tests are made are located at the universities of Michigan and Pennsylvania, the Smithsonian Institution, and at the Argonne National Laboratory in Illinois. The journal *Radiocarbon* carries the updated listings of test results.

While C-14 dates are solidly based, their plus-and-minus factor does not allow for strictly absolute determinations. And pottery cannot by itself provide more than a connection with a general period, although when it is found together with datable inscriptions or coins, its precision increases. On the whole, then, this means that archaeology has had to search for more controlled ways to arrive at absolute dates. Besides the items just mentioned, one of the most important means for dating archaeological material in Palestine has been through correlations with Egyptian data.

THE IMPORTANCE OF EGYPTIAN CONNECTIONS

The primary factor to know in regard to Egyptian chronology and history is that a valuable record was left behind by an Egyptian priest named Manetho. This priest, who lived in the late fourth century B.C.E., compiled a list of the pharaohs of Egypt from the time of its earliest leader, Narmer, to the days of Alexander the Great. Although the original was lost, Manetho's writing was quoted by others. According to Manetho, Narmer was the founder of the first of the thirty pharaonic dynasties, which he proceeded to discuss. The foundations of ancient Egyptian history, as these exist today, are very much dependent on Manetho's scheme of dynasties, although many corrections have been made, based on archaeological finds such as pharaonic lists that have turned up in excavations in Egypt.

The chronology of the first part of Egypt's history, the Old Kingdom, is still debated. Differences exist between scholars who hold to what is referred to as a "high" over against a "low" chronology. A high chronology represents somewhat earlier dates, while somewhat later dates are held by those who advance a low chronology. As far as Narmer is concerned, some scholars date the beginning of his reign to about 3100 B.C.E., while others are inclined to push this foundational date back to 3300 B.C.E.

Particularly important for Palestine during the First and Second dynasties have been examples of Palestinian pottery found in tombs in Egypt. The presence of this pottery probably occurred as a result of some kind of trade, and thus it is significant for the relationships between the two areas. Regarding chronology, the refined dates in Egypt help to give more precise dates to pottery vessels made in Palestine and found in Egypt. Thus, when this same type of pottery is found at Palestinian sites, the latter can be fixed into the scheme of Egyptian-based dates.

An example of Palestinian pottery found in Egyptian tombs of the first two dynasties was the so-called Abydos jug. This vessel type was clearly of Palestinian origin, but several examples of it appeared in the royal tombs at Abydos. The Egyptian examples have taken on great importance in correlating chronologies between Palestine and Egypt during the earliest period of Egyptian history.

Figure 3.1. Early Bronze Age "Abydos"-type jug from Bab edh-Dhra.

INSCRIPTIONS OF PHARAOHS

Beginning about 1500 B.C.E., Egyptian chronology becomes more precise. A key event for an absolute date is the military expedition of Tuthmosis III to Palestine. This expedition is detailed in a well-preserved inscription on one of the walls of the temple at Karnak. The Palestinian cities destroyed by Thutmosis are listed. It seems that a date of 1482 B.C.E. for the Thutmosis expedition cannot be far wrong, and if that is so, archaeologists are provided with some precisely dated events with which to compare evidence excavated at Palestinian sites named in the list. Thus at Taanach, Meggido, and other sites, archaeologists have argued for a correlation between the Late Bronze Age destruction levels and the recorded destruction caused by Thutmosis III.

Other pharaohs also recorded events in Palestine. On a different wall of the temple at Karnak the pharaoh Shishak I (Sheshonk) listed cities he destroyed on his campaign in Palestine. In the Bible, 1 Kings 14:25–26 refers to an invasion of Jerusalem by this pharaoh, and this is taken by biblical historians to be connected with the same events as Shishak's list. According to the biblical account, his invasion is said to have taken place in the fifth year of Rehoboam, Solomon's son. Egyptian chronology gives a more precise, absolute date of sometime around 920 B.C.E. for these events. The cities Shishak destroyed were thus most likely built during Solomon's time, so that this is one of the solid cross-references to Egypt for the dating of archaeological remains of the tenth century B.C.E.

It is evident, then, that by relating discoveries in Palestine to dates obtained from Egypt, a rather solid structure for chronology can be created. These Egypt-related dates often make it possible to specify biblical events with determinative calendar dates. Such work on the part of biblical scholars, Egyptologists, and archaeologists is of great importance for the study of the Bible, since the Bible itself did not locate events in an absolute sense chronologically. Names such as Shishak of Egypt, Sennacherib of Assyria, or Cyrus of Persia are mentioned, but no absolute reference points are given as to when these leaders lived. The biblical student soon comes to understand that biblical tradition did not operate with a developed system of chronology. The Bible's way

Figure 3.2. Temple at Karnak on one of whose walls Pharaoh Shishak recorded Palestinian cities he attacked.

of dating events and personages was entirely internal. No standard existed in terms of which events could be specified according to a broader chronology, linking past and present.

SOLAR AND ASTRONOMIC PHENOMENA
AND EGYPTIAN DATES

This is where the Egyptians made an unusual contribution to a chronology for those who would come after. Happily, the Egyptians attempted to connect events of their times with astronomical phenomena. They were acute observers of planetary and stellar phenomena, often recording these on the ceilings of tombs. They observed and recorded eclipses, and sometimes related events and personages to these.

One astronomical interest the Egyptians had was in the fixed star, Sirius, to which they gave the name Sothis. Their observations led them to conclude that every 365 plus ¼ days Sothis would appear anew on the horizon at dawn. This is known as the heliacal rising of Sothis, and it provided the basis for one of the first scientific efforts to establish a calendar. Since the common (or civil) calendar of Egypt was based on a regularized twelve months of thirty days each, with five days added at the end, this meant that the Sothic and civil calendars would differ by one-quarter day each year, adding up to an entire day every four years. Figuring this mathematically, it would then take Sothis 1,460 years (4 × 365) to once again be in a position so that the new year of the civil calendar would coincide with that of the Sothic calendar. These periods of 1,460 years are known as Sothic cycles, and the Egyptians recorded events in relation to them. Since modern astronomy can establish the dates of the Sothic cycles, it is possible to extrapolate from those points in obtaining absolute calendar dates for many Egyptian events.

EGYPTIAN CHRONOLOGY AND THE HEBREW EXODUS

Unfortunately, a key event in the Bible—the exodus of the Hebrew people from Egypt—remains obscure so far as its date is concerned. The biblical account in Exodus 1–15 is sketchy, and even though a number of Egyptian names and terms occur in the texts, it is not possible to be certain that they can be connected with a specific time or personage in the Egyptian chronology. The bulk of scholarship tends to see the pharaoh involved as Rameses II, the dates of whose reign are traditionally given as 1290–1224 B.C.E., although a recent proposal is that they should be lowered by eleven years.

EARTHQUAKES AND CHRONOLOGY

In addition to astronomical data used by Egyptians, a further natural phenomenon that has been studied for its dating possibilities is earthquake. Since Palestine is a region susceptible to tectonic activity, specific events of earthquake were often referred to in the written literature. One instance of earthquake is recorded in the Hebrew Bible (Amos 1:1; Zech. 14:5), but unfortunately most of the absolute dates available for earthquakes are from the last 2,000 years, so that earlier episodes are difficult to date. Archaeologists do find evidence of earthquake destruction, and the effort is thus made to match up such data with references in written material.

DATING DIFFERENT TYPES OF ARCHAEOLOGICAL SITES

We can sum up our discussion of chronology by saying that the type of site has an effect on the problem of dating. A temporarily settled site of the Paleolithic period will contrast greatly with a densely occupied urban settlement of later historic times. In the case of an early camping site, the only artifacts will probably be flints, and pottery might even be lacking. By contrast, an urban site will contain rich amounts of cultural data. Determining the time range for the first type would depend primarily on identifying and dating the flints, along with making C-14 tests of collected material. Neither of these would, however, yield a closely defined chronology, which is the reason why so much prehistoric archaeology is unable to date an occupation to within even several centuries, but must be satisfied with more general dates spreading over longer periods of time.

A complex urban site, on the other hand, will commonly contain information that can be more precisely dated. The special place of pottery has already been discussed. In addition to this, some of the datable cultural artifacts found at the site would include: imported pottery or artifacts that are closely dated in the archaeology of the country from which they were exported, such as Mycenaean wares from Greece during the Late Bronze Age; inscriptional evidence referring to events or personages, such as the cartouche of the Egyptian queen Tausert found at Deir Alla in Jordan; and coins found in uncontaminated strata of a site, containing information about when they were minted and thus serving to date the strata in which they were found.

AN ARCHAEOLOGICAL TIMETABLE

We conclude this chapter, then, by presenting the chronological framework with which archaeologists and historians of ancient Palestine work. This framework will be used throughout the remainder of the book, so it will be important to understand it and become thoroughly familiar with it. It is a chronology that has been worked out over the past century of archaeological work in Jordan and Israel.

This framework employs technological terms (*stone, bronze, iron*) for the early periods, while during later periods the nomenclature becomes that of the dominating Middle Eastern empires. The designation of periods by technological terminology was first introduced in a work by Christian Thomsen published in 1836. This Danish scholar proposed a three-age cultural development in antiquity: the Stone, Bronze, and Iron ages. Although this scheme is too simple, it has served usefully for subsequent chronology building. The vast amount of work done since Thomsen's time has resulted in much refinement of this basic chronology.

The best way to remember the chronology is to learn it according to the following eras or ages: the Stone, Copper or Bronze, and Iron ages, and the various empires. The following table would be acceptable to most archaeologists working in Palestine today, although some would undoubtedly make adjustments in some of the dates.

Finding How Old Things Are

Period	Dates
The Stone Age	
Lower Paleolithic	1,000,000 years ago to 120,000 B.P.
Middle Paleolithic	120,000–40,000 B.P.
Upper Paleolithic	40,000–19,000 B.P.
Epipaleolithic	19,000–8000 B.P.
Neolithic	8000–4500 B.C.E.
Early Chalcolithic	4500–3800 B.C.E.
Late Chalcolithic	3800–3300 B.C.E.
The Copper/Bronze Age	
Early Bronze IA	3300–3150 B.C.E.
Early Bronze IB	3150–3000 B.C.E.
Early Bronze II	3000–2750 B.C.E.
Early Bronze III	2750–2300 B.C.E.
Early Bronze IV	2300–2000 B.C.E.
Middle Bronze I	2000–1800 B.C.E.
Middle Bronze II	1800–1650 B.C.E.
Middle Bronze III	1650–1500 B.C.E.
Late Bronze I	1500–1375 B.C.E.
Late Bronze II	1375–1200 B.C.E.
The Iron Age	
Iron IA	1200–1125 B.C.E.
Iron IB	1125–1020 B.C.E.
Iron IC	1020–926 B.C.E.
Iron IIA	926–814 B.C.E.
Iron IIB	814–721 B.C.E.
Iron IIC	721–586 B.C.E.
The Empires	
Neo-Babylonian	586–539 B.C.E.
Persian	
Persian I	539–450 B.C.E.
Persian II	450–332 B.C.E.
Greek	
Early Hellenistic	332–198 B.C.E.
Late Hellenistic	198–63 B.C.E.
Roman	
Early Roman	63 B.C.E.–135 C.E.
Middle Roman	135–250 C.E.
Late Roman	250–360 C.E.
Byzantine	
Early Byzantine	360–491 C.E.
Late Byzantine	491–640 C.E.
Islamic and Crusader	
Early Islamic	640–1291 C.E.
Early Crusader	1099–1187 C.E.
Late Crusader	1187–1291 C.E.
Late Islamic	1291–1918 C.E.

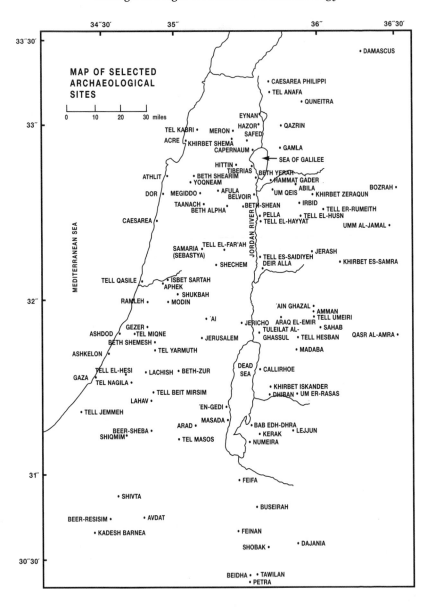

Figure 3.3. Map of Palestinian sites.

4
The Stone Age Occupants

The earliest archaeological remains of ancient Palestine take us back almost as far as it is possible to go in tracing the origins of human beings and their early cultures. Although modern paleoanthropological research has shown that the predecessors of today's humans most likely originated in eastern Africa, the archaeology of ancient Palestine has also brought to light data for the earliest periods of human development. This is because as early Stone Age people made their way from Africa toward more northerly latitudes, they sometimes passed through or settled in the region of ancient Palestine. What they left behind has opened up a rich area of investigation for archaeologists concentrating on these very early periods.

Interest in who the remote ancestors of the human family were is a rather recent one. Not until the nineteenth century did data in Europe begin to come to light that put this kind of study on a scientific basis. It was in the mountainous area near Santamander in northern Spain in 1879, and then later in 1940 in the Dordogne valley of southwestern France, that several well-known Upper Paleolithic cave drawings were discovered, giving rise to a fascination with and curiosity over the early people who produced this remarkable art. In France the discovery of Paleolithic stone tools in caves and in creek and river beds piqued the interest of researchers in the direction of investigating early humans. In fact, the names used for several of the Stone Age cultures found in Palestine are taken from type sites in France, such as Acheul and Le Moustier. The discovery of the famous cranium in the Neanderthal valley near Düsseldorf in Germany was another significant breakthrough, providing the name for a pre-human group that died out. Examples of the Neanderthal type

Lower Paleolithic	1,000,000–120,000 B.P.
Middle Paleolithic	120,000–40,000 B.P.
Upper Paleolithic	40,000–19,000 B.P.
Epipaleolithic	19,000 B.P.–8000 B.C.E.
Neolithic	8000 B.C.E.–4500 B.C.E.

have also come to light in Palestine, although a direct connection with *homo sapiens* is no longer held.

Even though Palestine was not the first area where prehistoric archaeology and research began to take place, it seemed inevitable that signs of early humans would begin to appear here as well. Over the years many Stone Age sites west and east of the Jordan River have been found. Ironically, therefore, it has been in the very land where the Bible was produced that some of the most significant data about early humans has come to light.

DISCOVERING PREHISTORY

Investigation of Palestinian prehistory did not at first attract many practitioners, and it has only been in recent years that concentrated work on these earliest periods has been undertaken in either Israel or Jordan. Various reasons can be given for this neglect. Since this type of research was bound to raise questions concerning the Bible's accounts of origins, many scholars tended to avoid this area of study. Other researchers were more interested in clarifying aspects of the Bible archaeologically, and thus they concentrated on later sites and periods most directly relating to the Bible.

That the extensive research devoted to biblical sites has produced invaluable results is an obvious fact, but that it has also resulted in a certain short-sightedness in archaeological research in this region is also true. Happily, this situation has been overcome, and the investigation of these earliest societies has now taken its place as an important part of the study of the area. It has also brought benefits to scholars concentrating on later periods, including those related to the Bible. Archaeologists have come to recognize that comparative knowledge of the wider picture of human culture and activity, from the earliest to the latest times, helps in understanding developments at any one particular period under study. This would include the later periods devoted to the Bible.

PREHISTORY AND HISTORY

Although the term *prehistory* is often used for research into these early peoples and cultures, the understanding of the past has sometimes been hindered by differentiating too sharply between prehistoric and historic cultures. Usually archaeologists or historians have used the term *prehistory* for early, nonliterate societies. The term *history*, then, has been reserved for those societies who by means of knowledge of writing began to record the events of their times, even though their records often were little more than chronicles.

This distinction, however, can have the effect of blurring the picture of development within a region such as Palestine. For example, is the practice of writing an adequate criterion for distinguishing cultures? Would this mean that the innovations of urban development during Early Bronze (EB) II and III that will be traced below (chapter 6) would have to be considered prehistory, since not one single written text from this period has yet been found in Palestine? And yet, the Early Bronze societies were well organized, participated in trade, and were specialized in a number of different activities. Defining where prehistory ends and history begins, therefore, may have more to do with the complexity of social organization than with the process of writing, although obviously studying a culture with written remains in hand next to archaeological data presents different challenges than studying a society completely on the basis of its nonwritten remains.

As they will be viewed here, the developments during the Stone Age were a significant segment of the long history of cultural activity in ancient Palestine. If the term *prehistory* is used for these periods, it should not be taken to mean that study of them is any less important than that devoted to more complex societies.

LOWER (EARLY) PALEOLITHIC PERIOD

The earliest Paleolithic inhabitants were hunting animals and gathering wild grains and fruits 600,000 years ago. We would not expect that remains of these early occupants would be as well preserved as those resulting from more recent human activity. In reality, much of the information that exists for such an early time has come from areas disturbed by centuries of erosion or from human activity, such as plowing. On the other hand, research on early occupations in rock shelters or caves has produced material preserved in a stratigraphic ordering. The period referred to as Lower Paleolithic is a long one, stretching from somewhere around 1,000,000 years B.P. (before present) to about 120,000 B.P., when the Middle Paleolithic began. Radiocarbon datings of successive levels in cave or shelter deposits have been determinative for these dates, as have refined studies of the kinds of stone tools produced during this long time period.

An important type of tool used throughout this long period was the handaxe. Roughly shaped from a core of hard stone or flint, this implement was often worked on both sides, giving it the preferred term by which it is called today, the bifacial handaxe. It seems certain that this implement was used for attacking and defleshing animals. When such bifacial tools are found by excavators, either in unstratified surface remains or in a rock shelter, they help determine the age of the deposit as Lower Paleolithic, although a more precise dating is dependent on C-14 tests of associated material. The bifacial tools are also hallmarks of an age that researchers refer to as Acheulean. The name is from a location not far from Amiens in northern France, where this Lower Paleolithic culture was first studied. The Acheulean culture is well represented in Palestine, spreading over much of the Lower Paleolithic.

Human remains dating to the Lower Paleolithic have been found in Palestine. During the 1920s a skull was discovered in a cave in the foothills on the northwest side of the Sea of Galilee (Kinnereth). Known as Galilee man, this famous human cranium has for many years been on exhibit in the Rockefeller Museum in Jerusalem. It is one of the most important prehistoric remains, and one of the earliest from Palestine. The skull is dated to approximately 120,000 years ago, placing it in the Late Acheulian

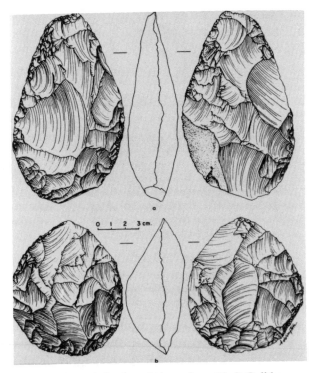

Figure 4.1. Late Acheulean bifaces from Wadi Qalkha.

period. The site of Wadi Qalkha north of the modern port of Aqaba in modern Jordan has also produced evidence of Late Acheulean artifacts, in particular, bifacial handaxes.

Possibilities exist that even earlier representatives of the Acheulean type will turn up in modern Israel. Some indications have already appeared at a site called Ubeidiyah, just south of the Sea of Galilee. Excavations here unearthed a wealth of animal remains, geological data, and tools fashioned by early occupants. Some of the remains suggest a date as early as a million years ago. Two teeth (a molar and an incisor) of a prehuman or hominid were found, along with several fragments of skull.

Both the cave site along the Sea of Galilee and the Ubeidiyah site demonstrate the importance of Palestine as one of the regions populated intermittently by early hominids and prehumans.

51

This local evidence is being studied in relation to east Africa, where the first developments toward modern humans apparently occurred.

MIDDLE PALEOLITHIC PERIOD

Dating to approximately 120,000 to 40,000 years ago, the Middle Paleolithic Age has been separated from the preceding Acheulean by means of a stratified succession of occupations at sites such as Kebara and Qafzah in Israel. Observations of changes in the technology of tool-making have also been important in determining the main features of this period. This culture is referred to as Mousterian, after the site of Le Moustier in southern France where remains of this type were first identified.

Flint tools and hunting weapons were important items in this culture, but in contrast to the large handaxes of the Early Paleolithic a greater number of medium-sized tools, some with a triangular shape, were made. The construction of the tools shows that time and effort were devoted to making them. A greater variety in types of tools also began to appear. As in the Acheulean period, rock shelters and caves were used, but evidence has also come to light that groups of families and extended families settled together in concentrated areas.

In Israel and Jordan alike a significant number of remains have been identified as Mousterian. In Israel major finds have come from caves on Mount Carmel, as well as from sites in Galilee and the Judean desert. In Jordan evidence of this period has been discovered in the Wadi Zerqa north of Amman, the Azraq basin in the eastern desert, and in an extensive region north of Aqaba. The caves of Mount Carmel were some of the first sites to be investigated for prehistoric remains, with British archaeologists working there during the 1930s.

One of the issues that has been much discussed is the relation of the human remains from Mousterian sites to the Neanderthal inhabitants of Europe. Recent restudy of Mousterian skulls, along with information coming from newer excavations, has suggested that the Middle Paleolithic peoples of ancient Palestine were not directly related to the Neanderthalers, but constituted a hominid group with greater affinities to modern humans than those belonging to the Neanderthal group. Thus these Middle Stone Age occupants have an important place in the emergence of modern human beings.

Since the Lower and Middle Paleolithic periods extended over such a long time, considerable change took place in the course of them. Paleolithic research is consequently concerned with major geologic and environmental shifts that occurred during these early times. It is also devoted to examining the differences in the animal and plant kingdoms between that time and our own, with the aim of understanding better the world to which Paleolithic humans were related.

UPPER PALEOLITHIC PERIOD

The period referred to as Upper Paleolithic began about 40,000 B.P. and continued to approximately 19,000 B.P. It is mostly contemporary with the European Aurignacian period, named after the site of Aurignac in France. The designation Aurignacian is consequently also used in Israel and Jordan, whereas Ahmarian refers to a related manifestation of this same general culture. As in the case of the preceding periods, the primary diagnostic feature was the stone and flint technology. Stone implements during this period consisted of long blades, burins (a tool used for boring), and what was apparently one of the earliest end scrapers. The latter tool type continued to be important well into the Bronze Age, and end scrapers dating as late as EB III are commonly found at Early Bronze Age sites.

Although Upper Paleolithic sites are not abundant, examples are present in both Israel and Jordan. One important site in Israel was discovered in the Nahal Ein-Gev along the eastern shore of the Sea of Galilee. Here the contracted skeleton of a female adult dating to this period was found. The Qafzah cave in Israel, mentioned previously for its earlier remains, also contained the fragment of an Upper Paleolithic human skull. In Jordan the Upper Paleolithic is represented in the Jebel Humeima region north of Aqaba. Sites of this period have also been appearing in the Negev and the northern part of the Sinai Peninsula.

EPIPALEOLITHIC

The Epipaleolithic period, dating from approximately 19,000 B.P. to 8,000 B.C.E., was formerly called Mesolithic, but Palestinian archaeologists have abandoned the latter term as misleading, preferring Epipaleolithic since it indicates the last remnants of the Paleolithic period. The most common feature of this period were small flint tools, called lunates because their shape was that of a half-moon. Their small size and unique form indicated substantial changes in the economy and social organization of the Epipaleolithic people. It is now evident that this period, which coincided with the warming trend of the last glaciation, set the stage for the significant social transformations of the following Neolithic period.

The culture of the Epipaleolithic was first identified at Shukbah in the Wadi en-Natuf northwest of Jerusalem, and thus the name Natufian has also been associated with this period. In recent prehistoric research in Israel and Jordan, this culture has appeared at a growing number of sites. In Israel, in addition to the Wadi en-Natuf site, are a number of remains in the Mount Carmel area. One of these, the Kebara cave (discussed above for earlier remains), has given its name to one form of the Epipaleolithic called the Kebaran culture. Also nearby is the el-Wad cave. In the Galilee area the site of Eynan has been an important representative of the same horizon. The same period has also been represented in Jordan, where Natufian sites have been found in surveys north of Aqaba. On the West Bank of Palestine Jericho had Natufian remains in its lowest levels.

The Epipaleolithic inhabitants continued a pattern of subsistence based on hunting and gathering. Recent evidence for this period, however, has shown that these occupants created small settlements and fairly durable campsites, and that they made real efforts at cultivating a number of plants. While the major breakthrough in plant cultivation and stock breeding occurred during the following Neolithic period, it now seems that the Neolithic was an outgrowth of earlier experimentation during the last stage of the Paleolithic.

THE NEOLITHIC PERIOD

The Neolithic period that began around 8000 B.C.E. is viewed today as a turning point in social organization and the way human beings have related to their environment. One prominent scholar, Vere Gordon Childe, has used the phrase "Neolithic

Revolution" to highlight these novel developments. The advancements made during this period included the introduction of agriculture and the practice of breeding animals. Both of these were to have widespread economic effects, resulting in major changes in the ways human communities settled and how they organized themselves. The period was thus an important stage in the emergence of complex societies, one that was to lead eventually to urbanization.

Archaeologists differ on the question about where and how these dynamics of Neolithic culture first emerged, and whether they developed at a single place or in several places simultaneously. Some have held that the point of origin of grain-crop cultivation, as well as the domestication of sheep and goats, took place along the hilly slopes of modern Iraq and Iran. Villages datable to this time, such as Jarmo, are viewed as early examples of such developments. The excavations at Jericho during the 1950s, however, produced new evidence for the Neolithic Age in Palestine. Jericho is the richest find of the Neolithic period thus far known in Palestine, although several other more recently excavated sites have produced substantial remains.

Earlier excavations at Jericho had already noted the presence of Neolithic remains, but it was not until the more recent expedition during the 1950s that this important period at the site was clarified. The Neolithic culture here began about 8000 B.C.E. continuing for several millennia until approximately 4500 B.C.E. The four major phases are commonly fixed in relation to the production of pottery. The first two produced no pottery and thus were termed Pre-Pottery Neolithic A (PPNA) and Pre-Pottery Neolithic B (PPNB). The subsequent two phases, involved in the first production of pottery, were called Pottery Neolithic A (PNA) and Pottery Neolithic B (PNB). It is now evident that pottery began to be produced in the Near East at about 6000 B.C.E., and although Jericho cannot be said to have been the place where it was first manufactured, the clear sequence from a Pre-Pottery culture to one that produced pottery is very clear at this site. Jericho has thus served as a model for the study of the Neolithic period.

The PPNA culture at Jericho is remarkable, but many questions about how to explain it still exist. Unexpectedly, the British excavators uncovered the earliest example of a walled settlement in Palestine thus far known. Accompanying this well-constructed walled settlement was a tower of extraordinary construction. Standing thirty feet high, the tower contained an interior stairwell of twenty-two steps leading to an opening at the top.

This combined tower and circumference wall are unparalleled at any other sites for this period. Their date in the PPNA period is indisputable since the stratigraphic work and recording of the excavators were superior. Jericho thus fits well as an example of the Neolithic Revolution. The PPNA settlement was agriculturally based, with barley and wheat apparently being grown as the main staples. Animals were also bred and used as a food source. At the same time, PPNA Jericho stayed within many of the traditions passed on from their Natufian ancestors.

A few signs existed that the people at Jericho were involved in trade. One was the presence of tools made of obsidian obtained probably from Anatolia (modern Turkey). A good possibility exists, too, that Jericho was a center for the export of bitumen from the Dead Sea, and this may explain the wealth of the city and its unique architectural features. The oasis in which ancient Jericho was located is still today one of the richest in the Jordan valley, and this also enhanced the developments that took place there. If one were to select a spot in Palestine where agricultural experimentation could be carried out, few areas would be more promising than this rich oasis region.

During the following PPNB period, a probable drier climate lessened the potential for development, and PPNB was thus not as spectacular as its preceding culture. Nonetheless, round brick houses built on stone foundations were associated with this phase. Especially important were the number of PPNB burials discovered. These burials have contributed much to the broader study of mortuary practices in Palestine. The burials were made in graves within the living area, often under house floors. Skeletons were flexed, but commonly the skulls had been removed and specially treated. The latter was done by applying plaster over parts of the natural skull, placing painted shells into the eye sockets to replicate human eyes, and applying a red paint to the upper part of the skull. These practices may have been related to an ancestral cult.

In real ways the introduction of pottery during PNA and PNB was a breakthrough for cultural change. The simple discovery that clay, used previously for structures, could also be used for making a variety of vessels, opened up a new technology with many implications for daily activity. Now an assortment of vessel types could be created for different functions, serving the eating needs of the population but also providing some of the first luxury items. The development of ceramic technology and art began in just this period, continuing through later periods to the present. Although the PNA and PNB cultures that began to produce these items were seemingly not as wealthy as their forebears in PPNA, they were nonetheless able to cash in on a continuing development through this period.

Concurrent with and subsequent to the Jericho discoveries, many other Neolithic sites have come to light in Israel and Jordan. North of Jericho in the lowland of the Jordan valley is the site of Munhata. Like so many of the Neolithic sites Munhata had evidence of a settled community whose round houses were of mudbrick on stone foundations. Also in Israel were the Nahal Oren site in the area of Mount Carmel, the well-preserved remains at Abu Ghosh just west of Jerusalem, and a recently excavated site in the Nahal Hemar.

In Jordan, too, a good number of Neolithic sites have come to light. One of these was Beidha, a PPNB Neolithic settlement located not far from Petra. Like Munhata, many of the living units at Beidha were round in shape. Evidence for the cultivation of barley was also found. Not far from Beidha was a recently excavated site, Basta, that has produced a rich amount of data for the Neolithic period. And near Bab edh-Dhra along the Dead Sea was the Neolithic site of Dhra, containing pottery dated to both PNA and PNB.

The most remarkable Neolithic site to have appeared to date in Jordan is 'Ain Ghazal on the outskirts of Amman. This extensive PPNA and PPNB site had well-preserved architecture, consisting of domestic buildings, as well as burials containing a similar kind of plastering and painting of human skulls as that found at Jericho. An extraordinary find at 'Ain Ghazal was a group of clay statues depicting human figures, the largest measuring as much as three feet high. The function of these statues

Figure 4.2. Plastered human statues from 'Ain Ghazal.

is still not clear but quite likely they served some sort of cere-monial purpose.

The Neolithic Age was apparently one during which some far-reaching trade relations between different regions were car-ried on. The most commonly found items at Neolithic sites sug-gesting trade connections were tools made from obsidian. Re-search has shown that the main source for obsidian during the Neolithic in Palestine was located far away at Goellue Dagg, southwest of the modern city of Nevsehir in Turkey.

THE BIBLE'S STORY OF THE FIRST HUMANS

As a follow-up to the data on early humans discovered by Pal-estinian archaeologists working at Stone Age sites, we might inquire whether the biblical authors who wrote the first chapters of the Book of Genesis in the Hebrew Bible were aware of any of this evidence for early humans in the very land where they lived. The answer is, obviously, that they were not. These writers came on the scene long after the various ages and periods that have been discussed here. At the same time they had no access to the means by which scientific exploration has brought such data to light. Apart from the curious list of nations in Genesis 10, their intention was not to deal with the origins of human beings and cultures, but rather to confront their readers with religious questions such as what human beings exist for, and what their destiny is.

Yet an interesting coincidence exists between the biblical stories and the archaeological picture of development during the Stone Age. During long periods from the Lower Stone Age to the beginning of the Neolithic in Palestine human beings lived as hunters and gatherers. Like the Garden of Eden in the Bible, nature offered these humans its resources. Then in the course of time humans began to till the ground (Gen. 2:15), which we have seen occurred during the Neolithic period.

During the Stone Age, then, populations were gradually developing specialized tools that would change their relation to their environment. The Neolithic Age introduced new advances that altered forever the ways human groups organized themselves socially. Such changes, beginning with grain cultivation and animal breeding, eventually opened the way to the founding of towns and cities. The lifeways of humans then would be very different from what they were in the long-ago days of the human past.

5
Life in the Early Villages

As people experienced the advantages of permanent settlement rather than moving about, they found their life patterns changing. The establishment of villages stimulated new forms of communal living that became even more complex as cities began to be built. At the same time, settled village life called for innovations in what archaeologists term "modes of subsistence." For example, since villages were dependent on a smaller area of resources, careful attention had to be given to farming methods. Although not all village farmers were aware of the need to rotate crops, it seems that some at least took pains to protect their fields from overuse. Where this was not done, production suffered drastically and the village organization tended to fall apart.

It is necessary to clarify the term *village* in order to differentiate it from a town or city. We define the village as a concentrated population whose settlements consisted mainly of dwellings inhabited by nuclear or extended families making their living by farming the local fields. Occasionally specialized structures might also have been constructed, such as a building in which flint tools were made or repaired, or a potter's workshop. On the whole, however, larger public buildings were unnecessary for the simpler type of community represented in the village.

Most characteristically, the ancient village was an open settlement, which means it did not normally have a surrounding wall with gates, although enclosure walls were sometimes used. The occupants usually lived year-round at the site, but many

| Early Chalcolithic | 4500–3800 B.C.E. |
| Late Chalcolithic | 3800–3300 B.C.E. |

examples of villages have been found, such as the Chalcolithic villages in the Golan Heights, that were apparently used only seasonally. Some villages produced items for export, although trading activities during the Chalcolithic period were not as complex as they were to become in the later cities.

THE SPREAD OF THE VILLAGE IDEA

Around 4500 B.C.E. villages began to appear on the landscape of Palestine as they had somewhat earlier in Mesopotamia. There were, of course, earlier examples of villages, such as some of the Neolithic settlements discussed in the last chapter. What sets apart the period beginning about 4500 B.C.E., however, was the continuous pattern of settlements of this type from now until the building of the first cities. Archaeological exploration has made a major contribution to the understanding of the village and its culture.

The widespread expansion of village life is associated with the Chalcolithic period in Palestine. This period is commonly divided into two phases: Early Chalcolithic from about 4500 to 3800 B.C.E., and Late Chalcolithic beginning around 3800 and continuing until 3300 B.C.E. The beginnings of Early Chalcolithic actually overlapped with the preceding Pottery Neolithic B, suggesting some continuity between those two cultures. A key site for this early phase is Shaar Ha-Golan, located near the point where the Yarmuk River joins the Jordan River just south of the Sea of Galilee. Excavations here showed a distinctive local culture containing some features of the Neolithic, but also representing the first manifestation of the Chalcolithic period. This evidence thus has given rise to the term *Yarmukian* for this Late Neolithic–Early Chalcolithic culture.

LATE CHALCOLITHIC FARMING VILLAGES

The peak of Chalcolithic culture occurred from approximately 4000 to 3500 B.C.E. The best known remains dating to this period were found at the extraordinary site of Tuleilat el-Ghassul northeast of the Dead Sea. Excavations at several low mounds at this site showed that a series of Chalcolithic settlements was built on top one another. Houses were constructed close together and often shared common walls. The walls were made of mudbrick, and were sometimes placed on stone foundations to protect against erosion.

The Ghassulians, as they have been called, left behind some remarkable cultural objects. Of particular interest was a group of masterfully painted frescoes found on the plastered walls of several buildings. Included in the motifs portrayed were geometric designs, and depictions of characters that may have belonged to the mythology of this well-off village people. These outstanding finds thus open a window into the religious beliefs of the Ghassulians, as do other data such as a building identified as a possible sanctuary, and molded serpents found on a number of pottery fragments. The artistically crafted frescoes at Ghassul point to the high level of achievement attained by some parts of Chalcolithic culture.

Ghassul was a large village whose livelihood was based on farming. Many other Late Chalcolithic sites in different parts of the country have also been identified as farming communities. A good example was Shiqmim located in the Beersheba basin of the Negev. Shiqmim was one of a number of Late Chalcolithic sites found in a survey along the Nahal Besor, although it was undoubtedly the most intensely settled. The excavations here have shown that a large village existed for a period of several hundred years. During that time successive settlements were constructed above one another, with the result that the cultural debris at Shiqmim was over three meters deep. It has been argued that the village was somewhat complex in its social organization, and that some people were recognized as being of higher status than others. To put it in archaeological terms, Shiqmim had a ranked rather than a strictly egalitarian society. If this interpretation is correct, then already during the Late Chalcolithic period a social system had begun to evolve that would characterize life in the later cities of Palestine.

In the Negev are also noteworthy Late Chalcolithic settlements. Three of them located near the modern city of Beer-sheba are known today by their local names of Bir es-Safadi, Tell Abu Matar, and Horvat Beter. Excavation at these sites has provided rich information about the Late Chalcolithic inhabitants. At all three sites a group of interconnected underground rooms had been burrowed into the natural sandy soils. Artifacts found in

The Late Chalcolithic period was characterized by an interesting combination of settlements in villages and pastoralism. While some of the population preferred to live in the former, others maintained a way of life long known in the region, the keeping of herds of goats and sheep. Archaeological evidence for the Late Chalcolithic and early part of the Early Bronze Age suggests that people representing these two lifestyles were dependent on each other for items each could offer. Pastoralists brought meat supplies to the villagers, and the village farmers made their cereals and other foodstuffs available.

these subterranean rooms showed that they had been used as living quarters, so that it was evident that some people during the Chalcolithic lived in dwellings below the ground. Many sheep and goat bones also appeared in the subterranean rooms. Cutting marks were found on some of the bones, indicating that they were leftovers from meals eaten by the occupants. Thus the people of the Beer-sheba sites were probably involved in herding animals at the same time that agriculture was practiced. The discovery of underground dwellings at Shiqmim has shown that also at this site some of the people lived as troglodytes.

Modern Jordan also has many sites dating to the Late Chalcolithic period. Very near the Syrian border in the northern part of Jordan is the exceptional ruin of Jawa in a remote region containing great quantities of basalt. On the basis of the pottery found at the site, it seems that this large settlement was founded during the Late Chalcolithic period. The occupants made use of the easy availability of basalt stone in constructing their houses and other buildings, and they also laid up an impressive enclosure wall around the settlement. A water catchment system was fabricated in the nearby wadi, with dams and collecting pools gathering runoff that could be used for agriculture, people, and animals. Given its well-preserved architecture, and its evidence for technology, Jawa is especially important as an example of a Late Chalcolithic farming and herding center. It was the expedition's work at this site that also finally clarified the unique "desert kites" found in various areas of the eastern desert of Jordan, and long known from aerial photographs taken over the

Figure 5.1. Chalcolithic pillar figurine from the Golan.

region. These large V-shaped structures made of stone must have been used to round up wild animals, such as gazelles, by chasing them into these traps. The desert kites were thus an important element in the subsistence mode practiced by the people at Jawa.

At Sahab, a suburb of Amman, a number of caves were occupied by settlers during the Late Chalcolithic phase, suggesting once more the use of natural caves or artificial underground caverns during this period. Surveys of the plain along the southeastern side of the Dead Sea have also shown that this area was exploited intensively by peoples of the Late Chalcolithic phase. Many sites occupied only during the Late Chalcolithic phase, and never used again thereafter, were recorded. On the whole the Late Chalcolithic peoples preferred the more arid or semiarid regions of Palestine, and thus the great concentrations of settlement during this period have been found in the Negev, the Jordan valley, and the Dead Sea area.

One other region of the country favored by Late Chalcolithic groups, however, was the rugged region of the Golan (Arabic: *jaulan*). The Chalcolithic evidence on this elevated plateau above the eastern shore of the Sea of Galilee is some of the most extensive to have come to light. Like their counterparts to the south, the Late Chalcolithic people of the Golan were engaged in agricultural production, as indicated by their farmsteads, of which many examples have been found. The Late Chalcolithic settlers combined their farming activities with pastoralism, taking their flocks into the open at certain times of the year and returning at other times to plant and harvest. A combination of agriculture and herding was often characteristic of the life of the Late Chalcolithic settlers.

The Golan settlers also produced a unique type of pillar figurine made from the volcanic basalt of the Golan, many examples of which have been found. The exaggerated noses on these figurines have been interpreted as symbolic of the power of the breath of life possessed by the god or goddess seemingly represented in the statue. The importance of the breath of life in relation to the deity is known elsewhere in the ancient Near East, and indeed is an emphasis in the early chapters of the Hebrew Bible (Gen. 2:7). These figures thus may also indicate something about the religion practiced by the peoples living in the farming villages of the Golan.

LATE CHALCOLITHIC PASTORALISM

In addition to farming villages, some of the Late Chalcolithic population also continued to practice pastoralism as their primary mode of life. This type of livelihood, still seen in the Middle East today, is characterized by greater mobility. Pastoralists are primarily preoccupied with the needs of their flocks, which include above all fields for grazing and springs for watering their animals. Since grazing areas become depleted after a time, pastoralists find it necessary to move from one locale to another, although in antiquity as today there were no doubt parameters defining their particular zone. Archaeological studies of pastoralism have sought evidence of the mobility patterns of particular groups, since pastoralists would tend to repeat season after season their routes into the grazing areas.

The pastoralism of this period is also suggested by the evidence from some of the contemporary burial grounds. One type of burial associated with the Late Chalcolithic Age consisted of placing human skeletal remains, once the flesh had decomposed, in clay receptacles called ossuaries, and then burying them again in large, natural caves. This means that bodies were originally buried elsewhere, most likely in the ground, and after decomposition the skeletalized remains were disinterred to be placed in these containers. Often these small clay ossuaries were shaped in the form of tents or houses, reminiscent of the structures that people lived in in their daily lives. That the burials in these containers were secondary, and that primary burial had taken place elsewhere earlier, suggests a pattern of nomadic or pastoralist existence in the case of the people making these burials.

A number of cemeteries along the coastal plain near Tel Aviv have yielded such secondary burials. One example was a natural cave near the Israeli town of Bene Barak containing receptacles of this type. No settlement associated with this cemetery was found, suggesting again that the burials were made by pastoralists. On the other hand, that several ossuaries were found in the burials associated with the village of Shiqmim suggests that this type of practice could also be associated with a settled or partly settled people. In the case of Shiqmim the question is whether pastoralists did not also, at certain times of the year, stay temporarily at this site, so that the ossuaries would have contained the remains of members of their group that had previously been buried elsewhere.

TEMPLES AND RELIGIOUS OBJECTS AT CHALCOLITHIC SITES

Two remarkable discoveries dating to the Late Chalcolithic period were made near the Dead Sea's western shore, and each of them apparently had something to do with the religious activities of the people in this region. The first of these is a large rectangular building still preserved on a hill west of 'En-Gedi. This building's architecture contains a number of features suggesting its function as a sanctuary. In front of the building is a courtyard with an installation where libations may have been poured out to a deity. The building itself is an elongated rectangle, with its doorway on the broad side. On the interior on all four sides are low stone benches built against the inside walls. The building's location provided those who came there with an impressive view over the Dead Sea to the east.

A further Late Chalcolithic discovery appeared at a site a few kilometers south of the 'En-Gedi temple. Here a cave was discovered in the high bank along the Nahal Mishmar. Because of its nearly inaccessible location, the cave was entered with a great

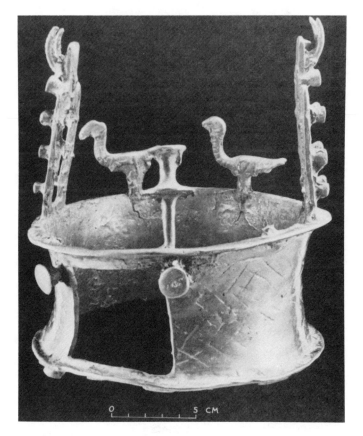

Figure 5.2. A "crown" from the "Cave of the Treasure."

deal of difficulty and risk by archaeologists. On the interior a hoard of unusual objects was discovered. Many of them were made of copper, and among the objects were maceheads, other objects resembling scepters and standards, and a piece shaped like a crown. Several flat-shaped objects containing holes like a Chinese-checker board were also found. These latter objects are intriguing but their function has still not been determined.

Since Nahal Mishmar is located about four miles south of 'En Gedi, one archaeologist has proposed that the objects found in the "cave of the treasure," as the Nahal Mishmar cave has come to be called, had originally belonged to the 'En-Gedi temple. Fearing perhaps that the precious items in the 'En-Gedi sanctuary might be confiscated, they were taken and hidden in the cave of the Nahal Mishmar. The Nahal Mishmar objects are so unique and impressive in their manufacture that it is difficult to think of their purpose as having been anything other than ceremonial. Thus their earlier association with the temple at 'En-Gedi seems a plausible interpretation. This cache of objects, then, is another highly instructive group of materials having to do with the religion of the Late Chalcolithic people. They parallel in their importance another special group of religious objects found at Bir es-Safadi, one of the Beer-sheba sites; here a number of figurines, carved from ivory, probably depicted divine beings.

FROM CHALCOLITHIC TO THE BEGINNING OF THE EARLY BRONZE AGE

The dividing line between the Late Chalcolithic period and the beginning of what is called the Early Bronze Age is not a sharp one. As will be seen, the first part of this period, referred to as Early Bronze IA (abbreviated EB IA), still had features of the Late Chalcolithic period, such as maceheads of Late Chalcolithic type. Some groups during EB IA were also pastoralists, like those of the preceding period. On the other hand, the EB IA phase differed from Late Chalcolithic, and had more similarities to the cultural developments that followed during the Early Bronze Age. It is best, therefore, to think of EB IA as a transitional phase.

One site with a great deal of material dating to EB IA is Bab edh-Dhra, located along the southeast plain of the Dead Sea.

During the later Early Bronze Age Bab edh-Dhra became the location of a sizable city. But earlier during EB IA, it was used mainly as a burial place, with no evidence of permanent settlement appearing during this phase. The EB IA burials at Bab edh-Dhra were of a type known as shaft tombs. These tombs consisted of two parts. A round shaft roughly three feet in diameter was cut vertically from the surface to a depth of about seven feet. Then from the lower part of the shaft a series of small, underground chambers was carved back into the natural limestone. Burials placed into the chambers were usually not fully laid-out skeletons, but consisted of a stack of human bones representing anywhere between two and eight people. The bones were placed in the center of the chamber, while the crania were set in a row left of the bone pile. Tomb gifts, such as pottery or bowls made from basalt, were lined up around the edges of the chamber. After the burials and accompanying items were placed in the chambers, the doorways were blocked with large stones cemented in place with clay or bitumen from the Dead Sea.

These secondary burials, like those of the Late Chalcolithic ossuaries, point to the nonsedentary lifestyle of the EB IA people at Bab edh-Dhra. The dead were buried at some place along the way, but then later moved to a special clan or tribal cemetery such as existed at Bab edh-Dhra. The reinterments at Bab edh-Dhra were probably made during seasons of the year when the pastoralists were in this area for grazing their flocks. Of some two hundred chambers that have been excavated, only a fraction have contained primary burials. And these are probably best to be explained as belonging to people who died during the time the group was staying at the site. Thus they had not been subjected to primary burial at another location and removal later to Bab edh-Dhra.

In addition to the burial practices that show similarities between EB IA and Late Chalcolithic, a popular item found in many of the shaft tombs was a bowl made of basalt. Although basalt was used during many other periods for a variety of purposes, this stone is an earmark of the Late Chalcolithic period. Maceheads were also found in many of the EB IA tombs at Bab edh-Dhra, and these can be compared with the many copper mace-

Figure 5.3. Human bones, skulls, and pottery found in an EB IA tomb at Bab edh-Dhra.

heads found among the objects from the "cave of the treasure" at Nahal Mishmar. Maceheads have also been found at many other Chalcolithic sites and are again a feature of this period.

Evidence for EB IA has been appearing in other parts of the country as well. In Israel a concentration of EB IA sites has been found along the coastal region of the Mediterranean, along the Nahal Besor farther inland, and in the Beth-shean valley and the Sea of Galilee region in the north. The picture has been similar to that at Bab edh-Dhra, namely that many groups were pastoralists, although they combined their pastoralism with either cultivating crops on their own or acquiring the latter from farmers associated with the smaller number of villages known from this first phase of the Early Bronze Age.

It would not be until the following phase, EB IB, that village life would again pick up in a dynamic manner. Thus it seems best to speak of some type of contraction, if not regression, during this transitional phase following the Late Chalcolithic period.

Factors contributing to the contraction could have included anything from climate and environmental changes, to economic, social, and political turbulence, and all of them seem to be indicated in some way.

Such contraction would also explain why certain developments that occurred during Late Chalcolithic were discontinued during EB IA. For example, the Late Chalcolithic period was a time when many copper objects were produced. We have already discussed the extraordinary hoard of copper objects found in the Nahal Mishmar cave. More recently excavations at Feinan along the eastern Araba in Jordan have shown evidence of copper mining here during the Late Chalcolithic period. And similar evidence had come earlier from the mining area at Timna near the Gulf of Elat on the Red Sea. Yet this metalworking activity ceased during EB IA. No sites dated to EB IA have as yet produced much in the way of metal, which must mean that this industry of the Late Chalcolithic period was not pursued during EB IA.

As a transitional phase, then, EB IA overlapped at both ends—with Late Chalcolithic on the early side, and EB IB on the later side. A new phase of village settlement began during EB IB, with many of the descendants of the EB IA pastoralists abandoning their older lifestyle for the challenges and advantages of the new villages. Thus the EB IB phase was an important turning point in the direction of the first urbanism of Palestine to be discussed in the next chapter.

6
The First Age of Cities

Beginning about 3000 B.C.E. the ancient Near East underwent an urban transformation that would leave this region changed forever. For the first time in human history cities began to be built in many areas of the eastern Mediterranean world. In Mesopotamia and Syria these new cities brought with them far-reaching cultural, social, and political changes. Palestine was also to share in these dynamics, which is the story of the archaeology of the Early Bronze Age in this region.

DEFINING THE CITY

Since we will be using the term *city* in this and following chapters, it is necessary to define this term in relation to the ancient Near East. Obviously, the ancient world had no cities of the size and complexity of the modern metropolis. Some large urban complexes, such as Ebla in Syria, achieved a size of more than a mile around the perimeter. And later during the Iron Age Nineveh in Mesopotamia had a circumference of some eight miles, but even this was far from the size of a modern city. Palestine's cities were even smaller. The largest Early Bronze Age cities such as 'Ai covered an area of about twenty-eight acres. This means that we must think in much smaller sizes when we consider cities of this early time.

Yet it is possible to use the term *city* for these early examples if we keep in mind a simple definition. In the first place a city will be understood as a compact settlement usually surrounded by a wall. Second, within this walled settlement a fair amount of diversity of human activity occurred, giving rise to a more complex economy, social structure, and political arrangement than settlements that were temporary or "village" in character.

Two terms related to the conception of a city are *urban* and *urbanization*. The term *urban* refers to features related to the city, such as its urban rather than village layout. *Urbanization,* on the other hand, deals with the process by which cities developed. It is this latter notion with which archaeologists of the Early Bronze Age in Palestine are particularly concerned, although they are also interested in all aspects of the urban settlements.

Tracing the process of urbanization in the Near East raises the question of whether the stimulus for this development came from within the society itself, or whether foreign influence contributed to it. The notion of internal stimuli would include the discovery of innovative technologies, such as those made possible by new implements for agriculture. This could result in spurring growth in the population, and alongside that the development of a more complex social system. The question of external stimuli is very much debated, and it involves the problem of whether or not the establishment of urban life in Mesopotamia and Syria, as well as in Egypt, may have influenced the events in Palestine.

Also important for studying urbanization in ancient Palestine is that we can often discern a cycle in which urban life thrives, then declines into a phase of nonurban life, after which there arises a new form of urbanization. This cycle is found during a number of stages in the history of ancient Palestine. We shall observe how it occurs during the transition from the Early to the Middle Bronze Age.

FROM VILLAGE TO CITY

The initial movement toward urbanization in Palestine began to manifest itself during EB IB. The village life of this phase differed greatly from the nonsedentary lifeways of the previous EB IA phase (see chapter 5). Thus, even though the settlements during EB IB were not yet cities, as expanding villages they paved the way for the transformation into urbanized settlements that followed later at the same sites.

The EB IB phase is known from a type of pottery found in a number of different areas of the country during this phase. This pottery was often decorated with groups of dark red painted lines, and thus has been given the name line-group painted pot-

Early Bronze IA	3300–3150 B.C.E.
Early Bronze IB	3150–3000 B.C.E.
Early Bronze II	3000–2750 B.C.E.
Early Bronze III	2750–2300 B.C.E.
Early Bronze IV	2300–2000 B.C.E.

tery. Some of the vessels on which this painting occurred were juglets with a single handle, juglets with two small ear-lug handles on the neck, and bowls with spouts. Another type of decorated pottery, called grain-wash ware, also occurred during this period, although it has been found at a smaller number of sites. These several types of EB IB pottery are easily distinguishable, so that this occupation can be traced at various sites where it occurs.

Variety existed among the EB IB villages. Some villages had round houses built partly into the ground, while others were large, open settlements consisting mainly of rectangular dwellings. At Arad in the Negev the EB IB settlement was the second earliest settlement, being preceded by a small Late Chalcolithic occupation. The EB IB houses were round. Caves were also apparently used. Farther north, Tell el-Far'ah had evidence of round houses built partly into the ground.

At many sites, then, the EB IB villages were followed by the building of the first cities. This suggests that the EB II cities were the outgrowth of a development that began during EB IB. At Arad the EB IB village was succeeded by the large, walled city of EB II. Jericho also had an EB IB settlement, following a long gap after its Neolithic occupation, and from this EB IB settlement emerged its EB II city. An EB II walled city at Tell el-Far'ah was built on the remains of the EB IB occupation, showing again the continuity from the EB IB village to the city of EB II. Also at Bab edh-Dhra the EB IB village of more than ten acres was succeeded by the first city at this site built in EB II.

THE CITIES OF EARLY BRONZE II

Many factors contributed to the expansion of the EB IB villages into cities. One of the principal forces was the growth of specialized groups devoting themselves to one specific skill or task.

Figure 6.1. EB IB line-group painted pottery from a tomb at Bab edh-Dhra.

This can be seen in the pottery of the EB II phase, which differed greatly from the simpler handmade vessels of EB IB. Sometime during EB II an early form of the potter's wheel called a *tournette* was invented, and this had the result that potters could now mass-produce vessels for different functions. The effect was that a special class of potters now became involved in this work. Similar specialization occurred in farming, in the construction work on the cities themselves, and no doubt in affairs of governance.

During EB II, therefore, true urban centers began to be built, incorporating within them these dynamics of specialization. Probably the best-known EB II city is Arad, located in the arid region of the central Negev. The excavation of Arad has been one of the longest and most extensive projects focused on an Early Bronze Age city of ancient Palestine. Work that has gone on for over two decades has opened up large parts of this EB II city, and much of it has been restored for modern viewing. Arad thus provides an excellent example of what a city of the first urban phase of ancient Palestine looked like.

The Early Bronze city at Arad covered an area of approximately twenty-two acres. It was enclosed by a wall more than

Figure 6.2. The Early Bronze Age city wall at Taanach.

two meters wide, from which were projecting circular towers located at approximately fifty-meter intervals. The layout of the city's interior consisted of planned sectors for domestic occupation, areas for industrial usage, and several structures used as temples. That trade was carried on with Early Bronze Age sites in the Sinai Peninsula has been shown by laboratory analysis of pottery from Arad and sites in the Sinai. Petrographic studies of pottery found at Nebi Salah in the Sinai showed that some of the vessels had been made at Arad, and that they were used to carry items from Arad to this site. Since the Sinai was also under the control of the Egyptians at this time, it is informative to have this kind of evidence. Other Egyptian evidence at Arad consisted of pottery of Egyptian style, and a sherd with writing referring to Narmer, the first pharaoh of the Old Kingdom.

It is possible that the political and military activities of the Old Kingdom in Egypt may have spurred occupants of these new EB II cities in Palestine into surrounding their cities with walls as a protection against attack. A wall made entirely of mudbrick was built around Bab edh-Dhra during this phase, with remains of it appearing below the much wider city wall of the EB III. The EB II city at Tell el-Far'ah was also ringed around by a mudbrick city wall, and one of the well-preserved city gates of this phase was found as part of this defensive wall construction.

Jericho also became a walled city during EB II, as did 'Ai in the hill country north of Jerusalem, and Megiddo in the Esdraelon Plain. Excavations at Taanach near Megiddo brought to light two successively constructed walls around the EB II city of that site. On the other hand, some EB II sites such as Gezer remained unwalled, and thus their relation to Early Bronze Age urbanization was not as significant.

One of the interesting things about the cultural remains of EB II is their uniformity. For several hundred years these cities flourished, but their culture changed very little. Pottery types, for example, retained essentially their same shapes during this long time. On the one hand, this phenomenon makes it difficult for archaeologists who depend on changes in cultural objects as signposts to draw conclusions about a period. But on the other hand this conservatism may suggest that the EB II phase was a time of considerable stability. Such a picture would fit well with the stability found in Egypt during the main part of the Old Kingdom period.

Yet things did change around 2750 B.C.E. It is not really clear why they changed, but all researchers working on the Early Bronze Age agree that at about this time a disruption occurred in the stable EB II societies. Perhaps there was some invasion. At Bab edh-Dhra it was earlier thought, for example, that the EB II city experienced destruction, and that the EB III city was built on the charred ruins of the earlier city. More recent work at that site has made that interpretation questionable. More likely, Bab edh-Dhra, like many other EB II cities, experienced internal social changes that led to the breakdown of the old order.

This breakdown, however, was not fatal because only a short time elapsed before new construction took over, leading to the peak of urban development at Bab edh-Dhra and many other sites during EB III.

THE CITIES OF EARLY BRONZE III

Many of the EB II sites were rebuilt and grew in size during EB III. Megiddo, Beth-shean, Jericho, Tell el-Hesi, Lahav, Tell Yarmuth, and Bab edh-Dhra are examples. Other EB II urban sites, such as Arad, Gezer, Taanach, and Tell el-Far'ah, disappeared at the end of the latter phase, and did not participate in the EB III urbanization.

Particularly striking is that the number of urban settlements east of the Jordan River increased during EB III. With a population of at least one thousand people, Bab edh-Dhra was a densely occupied site during EB III, and it was during this phase that it reached the height of its prosperity. Other EB III cities on the plateau in Jordan are Lejjun, Modowwereh, and in the northern part of Jordan, Khirbet Zeraqun and Tell el-Mughaiyir. Even these are only a handful of the many EB III sites known from survey to exist in Jordan, most of them still unexcavated.

One unusually well preserved EB III site in Jordan is Numeira, along the eastern shore of the Dead Sea. Numeira was occupied exclusively during EB III and never thereafter. It also had the good fortune of remaining untouched for millennia. No subse-

> So well built were Early Bronze Age cities that their ruins can be traced today. During the third millennium B.C.E. the impressive Early Bronze Age cities dominated the landscapes where they were located. At such sites as Megiddo, Taanach, Dan, Beth-shean, Beth Yerah, Ai, Arad, Bab edh-Dhra, Lahav, Tell el-Hesi, and many others, these walled cities with their gateways bore witness to a new type of urbanized lifestyle not before known in ancient Palestine. The *tells*, or archaeological mounds, that are seen today began to be formed as the debris of centuries collected above the massive city walls of the Early Bronze Age.

quent settlements were established at the site, and damage from later farming activity was minimal. Only natural erosion had modified the site. Thus, excavation provided a direct view into the EB III city just before its final abandonment. The fact that the entire settlement of Numeira was burned suggested that either earthquake or enemy attack had brought its end.

Like Bab edh-Dhra during EB III, Numeira was fortified with a town wall nearly three meters wide. Its gateway overlooked the flatland next to the Dead Sea below it on the west. Excavation of the interior of the city showed that different dwellings were linked together with common walls. Buildings contained rooms for living, as well as storage and cooking areas. A sanctuary was not found, but a tower on the east end contributed to the defensive capacities of the site. On the floors of many of the rooms were numerous items from the daily life of the EB III people, including barley grains, grapes, weaving tools, yarn, and sickle blades. In one case two sickle blades had been cemented with Dead Sea bitumen into a wooden or bone handle. Most striking were the skeletons of several adult males victims overtaken by the events that brought the city to an end. Their partly burnt skeletal remains were embedded in ash west of the tower.

Since Numeira is located approximately eight miles south of Bab edh-Dhra, and since its layout paralleled that of Bab edh-Dhra during EB III, the people of the two sites were undoubtedly related. Their relation was made clearer by petrographic analysis of several pottery vessels found in the EB III tombs at Bab edh-Dhra. The analysis showed that these vessels were made from sandy clay found near Numeira. The fact, then, that Numeira pottery was found in tombs at Bab edh-Dhra led to the conclusion that the occupants of Numeira sometimes brought their dead to be interred at Bab edh-Dhra, probably because the extremely stony topography around Numeira was unsuitable for a cemetery at this site.

These examples of EB III sites in Jordan indicate also that favorable climatic conditions fostered urban growth. Evidence recovered by the Dead Sea expedition showed a somewhat greater annual rainfall at this time in comparison to the late third millennium B.C.E. Resources were plentiful, including newly domesticated grains such as wheat and barley. Strides forward were made in cultivating fruit crops. In addition, the Early Bronze Age people colonized many previously unused areas of the country, and thus soils in those areas were rich. People living during this time apparently experienced a high level of physical comfort. Military invasions and destructions were few over the course of several hundred years. Human skeletal remains show a people with comparatively good health. Life expectancy for males was approximately sixty years, and for females a few less than that. Infant mortality, while present, was not overly excessive. And widespread plagues apparently did not occur, at least through most of EB III.

THE MAIN FEATURES OF EARLY BRONZE AGE URBAN SETTLEMENT

How then should the Early Bronze Age urban civilization on both sides of the Jordan River be characterized? In contrast to the great cities of the Mesopotamian river valley during the third millennium B.C.E., Palestine's urban population developed according to what was available in its own local resources. While these resources could not approach those of Mesopotamia and Egypt, they allowed a thriving local form of urbanization to develop.

As far as contacts with the outside world were concerned, Palestine's geography and more limited resources curtailed its outside connections. While it is possible to speak of trade during this period, the exchange system of the Early Bronze Age was a simple, more limited one. This is no doubt one reason why not a single written text of any sort dating to this period has been discovered in Palestine. Trade transactions were not widespread and determinative enough to have spurred literacy. Thus the Early Bronze population remained a nonliterate, albeit semicomplex, community. Its trading activities hardly reached the level of those found at Ebla, where economic tablets have shown a major trading enterprise during the third millennium B.C.E. Thus, while the Early Bronze Age settlements of Palestine were cities, they were provincialized expressions of urbanization.

One unique type of pottery, whose appearance during EB III has raised the question of possible widespread trade, is the Khirbet Kerak ware. This pottery is usually found in a dark red or black color, or a combination of the two, and it is highly burnished. The first examples of it were found in the excavations at Beth Yerah (also known by its Arabic name, Khirbet Kerak, after which the pottery was called) near the Sea of Galilee. The pottery has subsequently turned up at many other sites, particularly in the north of Palestine. The original production of this pottery has been traced to Anatolia (modern Turkey), suggesting that it may have come into Palestine as an element in commercial activity involving Palestine and its northern neighbor. In the course of time local potters in Palestine also learned how to make this type of pottery.

As far as political organization during EB III was concerned, most likely a chieftain or even a king headed the Early Bronze Age cities of Arad, Jericho, Tel Yarmuth, Beth Yerah, Bab edh-Dhra, and others. A very large charnel house at Bab edh-Dhra, containing jewelry made of fine gold, suggested the type of objects owned by wealthier members of this society. The layouts of the Early Bronze cities also indicated a certain amount of complex organization. For example, at Beth Yerah a group of oversized grain bins associated with a massive granary building suggested that these were probably government-owned facilities. Different groups in the society played different roles. Temples or sanctuaries were prominent, sometimes with features reminiscent of Mesopotamia. In them a class of religious specialists probably functioned.

A number of buildings identified as EB III temples have been found. Normally these structures were long buildings with a rectangular shape. The entry into the building was usually on the broad side. In several cases a podium or platform against the wall suggested that a statue of a deity must have stood on the interior, although no examples of statues have been found in the ruins of these temples. During EB III many of these buildings had several wooden pillars resting on stone pedestals across the center of the structures. And in a number of cases round or partly round altars were found in the court areas near the buildings. Examples of such EB III temples have been found

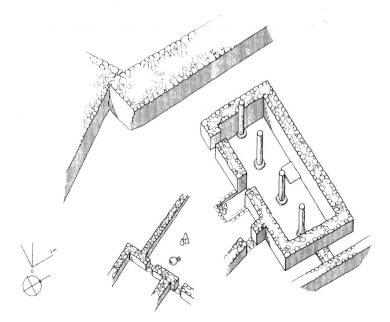

Figure 6.3. Axonometric drawing of an Early Bronze Age temple at Tel Yarmuth.

in prominent areas of Megiddo, 'Ai, and Tel Yarmuth in Israel, and at Bab edh-Dhra and Khirbet Zeraqun in Jordan.

EB III society witnessed the contributions of a number of specialists. Of particular importance for the many construction projects of this period were engineers. Techniques employed in building defensive walls and structures on the city interior indicated that people with special skills were active in this work. The abundance of finely made Early Bronze Age pottery was produced by specialists in the craft of ceramic production. At EB III Tell el-Far'ah a kiln was discovered, giving insight into the manufacturing techniques of potters. Other members of the community were engaged as tool producers, sharpening (the technical term is *retouching*) the flint blades used for harvesting. Still others were brickmakers and bricklayers. And a certain group took charge of constructing the well-made tombs of this period, such as the charnel houses at Bab edh-Dhra.

THE COLLAPSE OF URBANISM IN EARLY BRONZE IV

This system of urban organization eventually experienced a severe trauma. The data for the end of EB III and the successive EB IV settlements, especially in Jordan, have shown that the whole urban system began to collapse at the end of EB III. Although not quite of the magnitude of a decline and fall in Edward Gibbon's famous phrase, this period experienced one of the major breakdowns in all of antiquity.

The decline of Early Bronze civilization left its mark across the landscape of Palestine. The evidence from EB III cities such as Jericho, Megiddo, Beth-shean, Bab edh-Dhra, Numeira, and many others, however, has shown that these cities did not cease to exist simultaneously. The process apparently stretched over a period of at least a hundred years. The causes also varied. In some cases environmental problems, such as decline in rainfall, contributed to the blight upon urbanization that occurred. Overuse of agricultural lands in the face of larger populations during EB III also resulted in some cases in serious degeneration of resources.

Whether any kind of military activity was involved in these events seems less likely, although the question is still being discussed. The various areas of ancient Palestine were all passing through a time of unrest during late EB III. In fact, in the Near East generally this was a time of turbulence. Egypt's Old Kingdom went into decline and an Intermediate Period of cultural regression set in. Mesopotamia witnessed the collapse of its early Sumerian cities, while in Syria Ebla felt the blow of invasion by either Sargon the Great or Naram-Sin.

The discussion of events in Palestine between 2350 and 2100 B.C.E. has centered on the question whether the EB IV population played any role in the destruction of the EB III cities. Some scholars have identified the people of EB IV (a phase sometimes referred to as Intermediate EB-MB or MB I) with the nomadic populations known in texts from Mari in Syria. They contend that the numerous EB IV shaft tombs, with an absence of EB IV settlements, would argue for a nomadic people returning during this phase. That picture would fit well with the peoples described in the Mari texts. It has been proposed, therefore, that some of these groups set out on a widespread migration to the south, during which they overran Palestine, assaulting its EB III centers and bringing them one by one to an end. They then set up their own encampments, but since they were nomadic they did not establish large urban settlements in the same way as the EB III population before them.

More recent excavations, however, have shown that some permanent settlements were constructed by the EB IV people. One notable EB IV settlement was that excavated at Khirbet Iskander in Jordan. This EB IV settlement was enclosed by a solid wall and also contained a well-constructed gate. Bab edh-Dhra also had an EB IV settlement, although this was built away from the ruins of the earlier EB III city. The evidence from Jordan thus suggests that in this region a number of substantial EB IV settlements were built. The picture in the Negev in Israel may not be greatly different, since also here the EB IV people had built some apparently permanent or semi-permanent settlements such as the one at Beer Resisim.

Figure 6.4. EB IV structures with pillars at Beer Resisim.

We are left, then, to choose among a number of alternatives for explaining the end of the EB III urban centers and the succeeding EB IV phase. One is that serious environmental events occurred in the latter part of EB III, coupled with human overload on the local ecology. Such pressures, it is assumed, would have led to the disintegration of the cities. As a result, some occupants went into the desert regions of the Negev, reverting to a pastoralist life of herding sheep and goats. Others went to Transjordan to establish, together with the dispersed peoples of EB III cities there, the new form of life associated with EB IV. According to this explanation the EB IV period represented a continuation of the preceding population and culture of EB III.

A second explanation follows a different direction. It interprets the demise of the EB III cities as having occurred by a movement of peoples coming from Syria to the south. In search of new lands on which to live, these people entered Palestine toward the end of EB III. They were primarily a nomadic people, but they also possessed weaponry such as daggers and javelins, with which they were able eventually to displace the occupants of the EB III cities.

Regardless of which explanation is more correct, or whether both were involved, for some two hundred years the EB IV peoples settled on both sides of the Jordan Rift. Then at approximately 2000 b.c.e. their activities and settlements also ceased. This time the causes appear to have been to a large degree environmental, exacerbated by a period of seriously diminished rainfall that devastated the Dead Sea region and other areas. The EB IV settlements fell into decline, and soon were completely abandoned, a phenomenon characteristic of EB IV sites everywhere they are found on either side of the Jordan River.

7
The Second Age of Cities

As the environmental conditions that helped to bring about the end of the EB IV cultures improved, the land became open to new possibilities. People began to move back to some of the same sites on which the Early Bronze cities had once stood. New urban centers were built above the ruined rubble of the earlier cities, and new locations that had never before been inhabited were settled for the first time. This flourishing time of rejuvenated city building was concentrated mainly west of the Jordan River, while in Transjordan the road to recovery following the Early Bronze Age took a longer time. This was the beginning of what archaeologists have termed the Middle Bronze Age.

SUBDIVIDING THE MIDDLE BRONZE AGE

In dealing with the Middle Bronze Age we note that scholars are not agreed on terminology. This may seem a bit confusing, but it is necessary to know the discrepancies between the labels used when reading discussions of this period. At the moment a consensus is emerging to use Middle Bronze I, II, and III (MB I, II, and III) for the phases of this period, following the end of EB IV of the previous period. These designations are supplanting older terms, according to which the end of the Early Bronze Age was awkwardly called MB I, and the several phases of the Middle Bronze Age were seen to begin with MB IIA, continuing with MB IIB and MB IIC. It will be seen in the second part of this chapter that the Late Bronze Age has fewer such problems.

Middle Bronze Age civilization was born about 2000 B.C.E., beginning with the MB I phase, and continuing into the period of city building during MB II. The new urbanization that occurred during this period would continue for four and a half centuries before temporarily falling apart toward the end of the sixteenth

Middle Bronze I	2000–1800 B.C.E.
Middle Bronze II	1800–1650 B.C.E.
Middle Bronze III	1650–1500 B.C.E.
Late Bronze I	1500–1375 B.C.E.
Late Bronze II	1375–1200 B.C.E.

century B.C.E. Even then this hardy civilization would not die, however, and soon a further urbanization during the Late Bronze Age, not as impressive as the preceding one, would appear about 1500 B.C.E., continuing until approximately 1200 B.C.E.

THE CANAANITES

With the Middle Bronze Age we are dealing with a people known historically as Canaanites. They are identified with the people called by the same name in the Bible, where the land in which they lived is also called the land of Canaan. Egyptian writings dating to the Middle and Late Bronze ages also refer to Palestine at this time as the land of Canaan.

Since the inhabitants of the previous Early Bronze Age cities were most likely also Canaanites, it seems reasonable to assume that some of the descendants of those earlier inhabitants had not forgotten the old walled cities of the Early Bronze Age, even though those settlements were in ruins. Such memories of the old cities may have been one of the stimuli prompting the Middle Bronze settlers to return to urban life. Other factors such as population growth, better climatic conditions, the discovery of new resources, and the cultivation of new technologies also motivated the people of the Middle Bronze Age to move back again to many of the older sites.

Where this new urbanization first began to appear is not clear, but it seems that the coastal plain along the Mediterranean was from early on a principal area of Middle Bronze Age settlement. Soon, however, the Middle Bronze sites came to be established in many areas west of the Jordan River. Only a few were established east of the Jordan River, and those were smaller in size and less dense in population than the settlements west of the river. The land of Canaan thus came increasingly to be identified with the land west of the river. This is also the way the land of Canaan is described in the Bible (Gen. 10:18–20).

CITIES OF THE MIDDLE BRONZE AGE

Of the MB I sites that have been excavated, one of the most impressive is located a few miles east of Tel Aviv. The mound, known as Ras el-Ain, has been identified as ancient Aphek, mentioned in documents of the second millennium B.C.E., and known to be important also in biblical times. Aphek's location at the headwaters of the Yarkon River gave it an optimum advantage. Following an Early Bronze occupation that also left remains at the site, Aphek grew into a major city. Excavations have revealed that Aphek was established toward the early part of the Middle Bronze Age, and that it continued into later phases of the period.

A defensive wall 2.5 meters wide enclosed Aphek through most of the Middle Bronze Age. Particularly important was the discovery of a multi-roomed palace containing pottery and objects dating to MB I. Surveys of the region also found that other MB I sites were situated not far from Aphek. Since these outlying settlements must have depended on Aphek for resources and defense, this too indicates the importance Aphek had as an economic and political center.

In addition to Aphek, other sites west of the Jordan River have yielded evidence of this same MB I culture, along with its continuation into MB II. Megiddo, along the Esdraelon Plain, is one of these. Many examples of dark-red, burnished jugs typical of MB I and MB II were found at Megiddo, although the settlement during this time was apparently not a large one. The opposite seems to have been the case at Tell Balata, identified with biblical Shechem. The first city on the mound of ancient Shechem was established during late MB I or early MB II, and this was only the first phase of what would be a much expanded city during MB III. During MB III the massive fortification wall that still encircles the ruins of Tell Balata today was constructed. It has been calculated that this wall stood ten meters high, and that its base was more than twenty-five meters wide. At least one gate was also built as part of Shechem's fortification system.

In the Negev, Tel en-Nagila was also a fortified Middle Bronze site, with pottery dating to the latter part of MB I and MB II. In

Figure 7.1. The Middle Bronze Age East Gate at Shechem.

the central hill country an occupation dating to MB I and to MB II was found at Tell el-Far'ah, although this was not a major settlement. Farther north an outstanding example of an arched, mudbrick gateway dating to MB II was found at Tell Dan, while north of Haifa an MB II palace with an exceptionally well preserved painted plaster floor with Minoan motifs like those found in Crete came to light at Tel Kabri. A similar Middle Bronze arched gateway has now been uncovered at Ashkelon.

The MB I and II periods thus saw an accelerating development of new urbanization. The development of tin-bronze, by which tin was added to copper to make a better metal, stimulated the revival of the period. Increasingly the urban sites were walled, suggesting that Palestine's place on the international scene had been strengthened, and that an internal defense system was needed. By the time of the final phase of this period in MB III, Palestine had reached the height of its growth and prosperity.

Numerous sites with MB III material highlight the importance of this phase. Even in Transjordan, where MB I and II evidence is sparse, an increasingly greater number of MB III sites have begun to come to light through recent exploration.

Many of the large tells of ancient Palestine contain remains that can be dated to MB III. Taanach, in the upper part of the hill country along the edge of the Esdraelon Plain, is an example. Following the abandonment of this city early in EB III, the site was again occupied during MB III. A wall was built around the city, and numerous structures, including a large palace-like building, were constructed within.

The imposing mound of Tell Gezer at the southwest edge of the Shephelah also had an impressive MB III city. Excavations revealed a gate and a city wall, the latter reinforced with one of the impressive MB III protective ramparts called a *glaçis*. This type of earthwork was made up of soils and stones thrown up against the exterior of the city wall. Although such a protective device had been used earlier on some of the cities of the Early Bronze Age, the glacis was perfected during the Middle Bronze Age, and some of the outstanding examples date to MB III. Gezer's MB III glacis consisted of compacted layers of soil and stone, with each layer spliced into the one below it. These ramparts were most likely designed to protect the city walls against attack by invaders who would attempt to undermine the city wall in their efforts to force entry into the city.

As MB III urbanization began to spread to Jordan, this depleted area also began to come to life again. Recent archaeology in Jordan has brought about a new perspective on this period. Earlier, it had been concluded that during the Middle Bronze Age Jordan was devoid of cities or villages, and that it had fallen primarily under the domination of nomadic groups. But as more surveys and excavations have been undertaken in Jordan, it has become apparent that this area too did not remain untouched by the advancement of MB III culture. Tell el-Hayyat in the Jordan valley has yielded the best material found anywhere for a succession of temples dating from MB I through MB III. On the western side of the Jordan River Jericho was a formidable city during MB III, and this same site has also produced some of the best preserved Middle Bronze Age tombs.

The growth of this Middle Bronze Age urbanism could not have taken place without an effect upon the environment. Where the large cities were built, forests were cleared for obtaining building materials and for making open land available for cultivation. Thus the activities of the Middle Bronze Age urban sites, like those of the preceding Early Bronze Age, left their mark on the landscape of Palestine, and later ages would inherit the kind of environment that the Middle Bronze Age inhabitants left behind.

The religion of the Middle Bronze Age is indicated by the temples found at some of the major sites. Megiddo, Shechem, and Hazor all had temples dating to this period, and the succession of Middle Bronze temples at Tell el-Hayyat showed a number of architectural changes from one phase to the next that probably also had religious significance. Although no other Middle Bronze Age sites have contained anything like them, the large standing stones found in an open area of Gezer accompanied a ceremonial activity of some sort, perhaps religious or political. Stones were used in this manner during the latter part of the Early Bronze Age, at Bab edh-Dhra, Lejjun, and Ader in Jordan, so the practice at Gezer may have been a carryover from practices of the Early Bronze Age. It was also during the Middle Bronze Age that terracotta figurines measuring between ten and twenty centimeters in height were made in great numbers. These figurines have been found in most of the excavations, and they continued to be made during the Late Bronze and Iron Ages. Earlier examples of a similar type of figurine were found in EB IA tombs at Bab edh-Dhra.

MIDDLE BRONZE AGE POTTERY

Pottery is important for differentiating the several phases of the Middle and Late Bronze ages. Early in MB I a new technique was already evidenced in the pottery-making industry. In contrast to the preceding EB IV phase, when pottery was often handmade and more crudely fashioned out of less purified clays, the pottery in MB I was made from clays whose impurities were cleansed by a process called *levigation*. This process involved placing the clay in water, allowing small stones and impurities to wash out. The finer clay made possible the construction of jugs and juglets with thinner walls than in earlier pottery, but also vessels that were stronger since they were fired at higher temperatures. A globe-shaped jug of this period was often treated with a dark-red slip and burnished to the point of polish. Among the finest vessel types was the MB I bowl made with sidewalls that contained a sharp angle called a *carination*. This distinctive feature became so popular that it continued to be included on bowls through the rest of the Middle Bronze period. Even during the Late Bronze Age bowls still had this feature.

An addition to this popular carinated bowl was the high ring base that also became popular during MB II. Many examples of an elegant bowl with a base of this type have been found in excavations containing materials from this period. The great numbers of them in MB II tombs at Jericho, Gibeon, and other sites, are an indication of their importance, since they were chosen as a special item to be interred with the deceased.

Figure 7.2. Middle Bronze Age goblet with high ring base from Jericho.

What made the production of fine Middle Bronze pottery possible was the introduction of the fast potter's wheel at about 2000 B.C.E. As noted in the previous chapter, Early Bronze Age potters used a slow-turning device known as a *tournette*. Examples of Early Bronze Age tournettes have come from Bab edh-Dhra and other sites. The tournette consisted of a flat disk with a small projecting cone on the underside that was inserted into a base containing a socket. With a hump of clay placed on the disk, the potter could turn the latter with the hand, or, more cumbersomely, with the foot. When the disk was turned by hand the potter could only use one hand to shape the vessel. Yet the technique did improve pottery-making, and the slow-wheel marks on EB II and III pottery indicate the gains made over the earlier practice of pottery made from coils.

With the introduction of the fast wheel in MB I, both hands of the potter were freed to construct the vessels. The new wheel consisted of a disk connected by a long shaft to a lower wheel that could be turned with the feet. This sophisticated instrument made possible the introduction of the novel ideas in pottery shapes that characterized the ceramic art of the Middle Bronze period. Such inventiveness gives us an insight into the cultural dynamism of this civilization.

THE INTERNATIONAL RELATIONS OF
THE MIDDLE BRONZE AGE

During the Middle Bronze Age Palestine for the first time stepped onto the international stage. Its involvements would not be as intense as they were to become during the following Late Bronze Age, but they were strong ones nonetheless. The main foreign influence on the Middle Bronze Age culture came from Egypt, which at this time was experiencing two major developments. The first had to do with the economic and defensive interests of Egypt itself during the Middle Kingdom. Pharaohs of the Twelfth Dynasty fostered a plan to exploit the copper resources in the Sinai Peninsula, and Egyptian garrisons were accordingly stationed in the heart of the Sinai. At the same time, the Egyptian presence began to be felt well into Palestine itself, even as far north as Shechem, according to one inscription.

A second development was the emergence of a people in Egypt called the Hyksos. These "rulers from a foreign land," as their name was understood by the Egyptians, had originally come from Palestine and had settled in the Nile River Delta. In the course of time they assumed control of the important city of Avaris, making it their capital. For approximately two centuries during the Second Intermediate Period they ruled over Egypt until they were finally driven out by the Egyptians of the early Eighteenth Dynasty.

Following the Hyksos expulsion, Egypt proceeded to assert its own control over Palestine. Already during MB III the Egyptian presence in Palestine had been strengthened, so that by the time of the Late Bronze Age Palestine had become, in effect, an Egyptian colony. Through these events the land of Canaan was drawn into a global political struggle that eventually proved fatal. By the end of MB III Palestine had become vulnerable to attack from the southwest. At Sharuhen the Egyptians defeated the Canaanite armies, opening the way for broad control over the region. A few decades later Pharaoh Thutmosis III attacked the cities of Palestine in one of the best documented events of antiquity. Recording his invasion in an inscription on a wall of the Karnak temple, Thutmosis III left behind the details of the final blow he delivered to the accomplishments of Middle Bronze Age civilization.

That the various Egyptian reprisals were traumatic for Canaan has been apparent for some time in the archaeological remains at Palestinian sites. Many of the MB III sites suffered destruction. At Taanach part of the MB III city was destroyed, while a similar picture was found at nearby Megiddo. Subsequently, in the Late Bronze Age, Thutmosis's assault against both cities left them in a severely damaged state.

These events meant that as the Late Bronze Age began a major rebuilding was required. The Late Bronze Age population included refugee families, who had survived the Egyptian attacks and were able to return to rebuild the ruined cities. They brought with them the traditions of the Middle Bronze Age and incorporated these into their efforts at reconstituting city life. Artifacts of the Late Bronze Age showed many continuities with the Middle Bronze culture, as did architectural units, such as temples, that adapted Middle Bronze plans. In many cases it was possible for people simply to repair the walls of the Middle Bronze cities rather than starting from scratch, and this was done at sites such as Taanach. Both the Middle and Late Bronze Age cultures thus were manifestations of the same people, the Canaanites.

LATE BRONZE AGE CITIES

In the Esdraelon Plain, Megiddo and Taanach emerged as well-built cities, continuing with rebuildings during several phases of the period. Both cities incorporated some of the older Middle Bronze Age fortifications into their new architecture. At Taanach engineers also cut a deep water shaft into the central area of the city, one of the earliest of such water-storage facilities yet discovered. Northwest of the Sea of Galilee Late Bronze Age Hazor was an imposing city with a solid defensive wall and a series of gates partially or wholly rebuilt in various phases of this period.

Hazor also had well-preserved remains of Late Bronze religious life. A Late Bronze Age temple at this site contained an outstanding group of standing stones, statues of deities, and cultic stands. Other Late Bronze Age temples were discovered at Megiddo, Beth-shean in the Jordan valley, and at Lachish in the Shephelah. Of particular importance was the Late Bronze Age temple at Shechem with its impressive standing stone that at a later time was apparently intentionally broken in half. The excavators proposed that the temple at Shechem might well have been the one referred to in the Bible as the temple of El-Berith (Judg. 9:46), and perhaps the fracturing of this Canaanite symbol may have occurred in connection with the Israelite settlement at Shechem.

THE LATE BRONZE AGE IN JORDAN

Late Bronze Age civilization also saw a revival in Jordan, as is now evident from an increasing number of sites that have been either excavated or surveyed. In the Jordan valley Tell Deir Alla was the location of a sizable Late Bronze Age city, while in the vicinity of Amman a large building dating to this period has been identified as either a temple or a crematorium. Late Bronze Age tombs discovered in the hills north of Amman at Umm ed-Dananir were found to have been built by people who occupied

Figure 7.3. Standing stones and statue in a Late Bronze Age ceremonial niche at Hazor.

a Late Bronze Age settlement in this region. The large mound of Tell el-Husn near Irbid in the north of Jordan has not yet been excavated, but broken pottery strewn about the site shows that it was occupied during the Late Bronze Age.

As more and more evidence of the Late Bronze Age in Jordan has come to light, an older hypothesis has had to be abandoned. This was that Jordan had no settlement during the Middle Bronze Age, and that it was also only sparsely settled during the Late Bronze Age. The interpretation was then advanced that it was during this period—when Jordan had no great cities—that the Israelite tribes moved through Transjordan before proceeding across the Jordan River. Since the country was basically free of cities, these tribes encountered little resistance except that which came from the newly established Iron Age kingdoms of Edom and Moab. These conclusions have had to be revised in light of the new evidence of Late Bronze occupation in Jordan.

In comparison with the great walled cities of the Early Bronze Age, the new cities of the Middle and Late Bronze Ages were not nearly as massive in their construction or even as large in total space. Yet they were impressive urban centers in another sense. In them the high culture of the eastern Mediterranean world found expression, as evidenced by the great variety of elegantly made art objects, including pottery. The exposure to the international scene that took place in this period stimulated such developments, but that exposure also made Palestine vulnerable in a new way.

Much like the preceding Middle Bronze period, the Late Bronze cities were probably city-states. Each city maintained its own administration, while outlying villages were often attached to its domain. Governance was in the hands of a ruling group, with a chieftain or king holding the highest position. Agricultural production concentrated on the cultivation of grains and fruits that had been introduced as early as the Early Bronze Age and thus by now were commonly utilized.

LATE BRONZE AGE POTTERY

The craft of pottery-making during the Late Bronze Age evolved from the traditions of the preceding Middle Bronze Age. Many changes were introduced that made this period a notable one for ceramic art in ancient Palestine. During the early part of the Late Bronze Age a decorative technique employing red and black paint was used to finish some of the pottery. Called "bichrome ware," this type of decoration was found in the form of geometric designs or images of birds. A variety of bowls and jugs was treated with this kind of finishing technique.

Somewhat later another kind of decoration consisting of dark brown paint on a whitened surface was applied to some vessels. Pottery with this type of decoration was termed "chocolate-on-white ware," and once more it has appeared at many sites dating to the Late Bronze Age.

Of particular importance were the considerable numbers of imported vessels that came into Palestine during this period. The Late Bronze Age, probably more than any other, was a period of imported pottery. A type of bowl called a "milk bowl" was imported from Cyprus. Its technical name is "white slip ware," and its presence at Palestinian sites has special significance for dating purposes, as well as for trade connections. During the same period a number of vessel types that originated in Greece made their way to Palestine, most likely arriving first at a coastal city such as Ugarit in Syria. From there they and the products they contained made their way inland. These Late Mycenaean wares are also good indicators of trade relations between Palestine and Greece.

THE INTERNATIONAL RELATIONS OF
THE LATE BRONZE AGE

Internationalism during the Late Bronze Age developed on a scale that surpassed that of even the Middle Bronze Age. Not only did the imported pottery referred to previously point in this direction, but written texts of the time suggest it as well. A city such as Hazor had contacts with several areas outside of Palestine, which is witnessed by the fact that the name of this city was found in inscriptions in Egypt as well as in Syria. Ashkelon in Palestine similarly had many contacts outside of the country.

During the Late Bronze Age a larger number of written texts appeared in Palestine, constituting some of the earliest written material to appear in this country. One such group at Taanach consisted of fourteen tablets written in Akkadian, the language of commerce during the Late Bronze Age, as it was earlier and later. These documents provided details of administrative concerns at this site. The fact that the Taanach tablets were written in the language of international correspondence is further evidence of Palestine's far-reaching connections at this time.

It was also during this period that the alphabet was developed, although some have argued that this may have occurred already during the latter part of the Middle Bronze Age. The discovery of this new and simpler means of writing opened literacy to larger numbers of people, thus also increasing the opportunities for economic growth.

The international contacts of the period were particularly strong in relation to Egypt. Egyptian objects found at Beth-shean in the Jordan valley showed that this large Late Bronze Age city had connections with Egypt of the New Kingdom. At Tell Deir Alla a cartouche of the Egyptian queen Tausert was found.

These items from Egypt are not unusual since one of the most important finds bearing on the Late Bronze Age in Palestine was a group of tablets discovered in Egypt itself. Known as the Tell el-Amarna tablets, these invaluable documents were found at the royal city of the pharaoh Akhenaten at Amarna, about two hundred miles south of Cairo. The letters, all written in Akkadian cuneiform, consisted of correspondence between the pharaoh and his Palestinian clients.

In these letters local chieftains at Late Bronze Canaanite cities expressed their concern over the weakening support of Egypt. They recorded that local dissidents called Apiru were causing serious unrest in their regions. The Amarna correspondence thus depicts the desperation of the Canaanite chieftains as they called upon Akhenaten and his staff to send help as soon as possible. The information is some of the most important we possess for Palestine on the eve of the Hebrew emergence in the land of Canaan. Among the dissidents mentioned in the tablets might well have been the Hebrews, although the two terms most likely do not correspond to one another.

BURIALS DURING THE MIDDLE AND LATE BRONZE AGES

Major cemeteries representing the Middle Bronze Age have been found at such sites as Jericho in the Jordan valley, and Gibeon just north of Jerusalem. At each of these cemeteries earlier shaft tombs originally cut during EB IV were partly cleared of their original contents and Middle Bronze Age burials were entered, accompanied by Middle Bronze pottery and artifacts. From these tombs has come an abundance of evidence for the Middle Bronze culture, as well as human biological data from the skeletal remains.

Unique also to the Middle Bronze Age, however, was the practice of burying human remains in large storage jars below the floors of Middle Bronze Age dwellings. A large group of such burials was found at Taanach, as well as at other Middle Bronze Age sites. At Taanach 90 percent of the burials of this type were children, perhaps indicating the desire of families to keep deceased children close to home. In the case of the several adult burials found in store jars, these obviously were placed into the jars secondarily.

During the Late Bronze Age inhabitants often sought out large caves for burial of their dead, although at Jericho Late Bronze Age burials sometimes continued to be placed into the old shaft tombs from the Early Bronze Age. Perhaps the largest Late Bronze burial group yet known was that found at Tell Dothan north of Nablus on the West Bank. This cave tomb contained a minimum of eighty-four individuals, an estimated one thousand pottery vessels, and numerous objects made of bronze, including eighteen daggers.

THE DESTRUCTION OF LATE BRONZE CIVILIZATION

Similar to what happened to a good many Middle Bronze Age cities earlier, many Late Bronze Age cities were violently destroyed at the end of this period. New settlements, then, were built above them but according to very different plans. This phenomenon was observed at Hazor, Megiddo, Lachish, and at a

Figure 7.4. Middle Bronze Age tomb at Jericho with wooden bowl and bed.

number of smaller sites. Occasional Egyptian raids on Palestine had already left Palestine in an increasing state of weakness and vulnerability, and now new threats were coming from a different direction. The Canaanite cities of the latter part of the Late Bronze Age were scarcely in a position to withstand some of the changes that were about to take place.

There was, in any case, widespread disruption throughout the eastern Mediterranean world at about 1200 B.C.E. For example, during the late thirteenth century, Mycenaean civilization in Greece was delivered a death blow by the Doric invasions. Serious disturbances also took place during this time on Crete, terminating the Late Minoan culture. The late thirteenth century B.C.E. was thus a time of unrest throughout the entire region, and it is evident that Palestine was not spared from similar turmoil. Whether any of this evidence for disruption at the end of the Late Bronze Age in Palestine was connected with the emergence of the Hebrew people in the land of Canaan is a debated matter to be taken up in the next chapter.

8
Two Peoples Contending for the Land

The settlement of the Hebrews and Philistines in the land of Palestine at about 1200 B.C.E. brought about another critical time of change in ancient Palestine. The details of the arrival of these two peoples are recorded for the Hebrews in the Bible, and for the Philistines in texts from Egypt. Each of these suggests that the political and social situation in Palestine at this time was a complex one. Not only were there Canaanites, Hurrians, and other minorities in the land, but now considerable numbers of the two new peoples were also making their appearance. An interesting question is whether this pluralism is reflected in the archaeological evidence of the period, and whether the Hebrews and Philistines are identifiable in any of the remains we have from this period.

THE PHILISTINES

The people called Philistines in the Bible were one of several groups in a class the Egyptians called Sea Peoples. They appear in Egyptian texts as Peleset, alongside several other seafaring groups. As with the other Sea Peoples, their homeland originally was in the islands of the Aegean Sea, and their language was non-Semitic. Furthermore, if the Peleset were the same people as the Philistines of the Bible, this would suggest that their place of origin was Crete, since the Caphtor from which they are said to have come in Amos 9:7 is most likely to be identified with the island of Crete. Yet these Peleset may also have had an earlier history in Anatolia, judging from their cultural traditions that point back to the southern regions of Turkey. Since Anatolia had begun to experience disarray somewhat earlier in the thirteenth century, the Philistine group may have moved from there to Cyprus for a time, leaving the latter under pressure from further population movements.

The biblical Philistines were among the Sea Peoples who attempted to gain a foothold in Egypt during the times of Pharaoh Rameses III (1182–1151 B.C.E.). Approaching Egypt on the latter's northern coast, the Philistines were met by the pharaoh's navy and defeated. One of the pictorial wall carvings on the temple at Medinet Habu in Egypt depicts Rameses' successful battle against the Sea Peoples. The portrayal on this wall is important not only for information about the battle, but also because it shows many details about Philistine armor, weapons, and dress, as well as the type of ship they used for plying the Mediterranean.

Following their defeat, the Philistine group withdrew from Egypt. Either Rameses III used them as mercenaries for Egypt's interests in southwestern Palestine, or they themselves settled along the southwest coastal plain, disembarking without resistance. In the course of time the southwest Palestinian coast came under their domination. Five cities constituting a Philistine league were given the names Gaza, Ashdod, Ashkelon, Ekron, and Gath. In the case of the first three the ancient names have continued to the present, and archaeological remains at them make their identification certain. Recent excavations at Tel Miqne also make it likely that it was the location of the Philistine city of Ekron. The location of Gath, however, continues to be debated. An earlier proposal that Gath should be identified with Tell Sheikh el-Areini has been abandoned.

PALESTINIAN SITES WITH PHILISTINE MATERIAL

As might be expected, the sites that have been identified with cities of the Philistine league mentioned above contain the greatest amount of evidence of the Philistine culture. At Ashdod,

Iron IA	1200–1125 B.C.E.
Iron IB	1125–1020 B.C.E.
Iron IC	1020–926 B.C.E.

excavations have revealed that Philistine remains are immediately above those of the destroyed Late Bronze II city. At about 1200 B.C.E. the characteristic Philistine pottery discussed below began to appear. This pottery continued in levels of occupation dated between the beginning of the twelfth and the end of the eleventh centuries. Thus for about two hundred years Ashdod was a prominent Philistine city.

Excavations at Tel Miqne (Ekron) have shown that this site was the location of a significant Philistine settlement. As a people from the Aegean Sea region, the Philistines brought with them a basically Late Mycenaean culture. During their earliest settlement at Ekron these settlers sought to continue some of the traditions they had brought with them. They produced an abundance of Late Mycenaean pottery types, but from clays that petrographic analysis has shown were from the nearby area. Thus the earliest Philistines at Tel Miqne were immigrants in the true sense of the word, attempting to carry something of the homeland customs with them. In the second phase of their settlement they began to make the pottery that has for a long time been called Philistine ware.

Not far from Tel Miqne is Ashkelon, where new excavations have been producing a picture similar to that found at Tel Miqne. As at Tel Miqne, locally made Late Mycenaean pottery was found in the earliest phase of Philistine settlement, followed by the distinctive Philistine wares of the next phase.

Other sites at which Philistine evidence has been noted lie along the coastal plain. Of special importance is Tell Qasile near modern Tel Aviv, where the excavators concluded that a temple rebuilt several times was a Philistine sanctuary. This building contained cultic objects and pottery that have long been taken to be an earmark of the Philistines. Some scholars have argued

The Philistines figure prominently in the Bible as a people with whom the early Israelites were often in conflict. An account of a war with the Philistines is found in 1 Samuel 4–6, which also describes how the ark was captured from Israel but then later returned.

against this interpretation, but in its favor is the prime location of Tell Qasile at the mouth of the Yarkon River. One could hardly find a better location for one of the settlements of a seafaring people.

Philistine pottery was also found at Megiddo in the Esdraelon Plain, indicating that the Philistines were in some areas of the country quite distant from their own region. Even more notable is the argument of the excavators of Beth-shean in the Jordan valley that a Philistine city had been established there. Although the archaeological evidence seems tenuous, the Bible records how the Philistines hung up the bodies of Saul and his sons on the wall of the temple at Beth-shean (1 Sam. 31:12). The question of whether the Philistines were at Tell Deir Alla on the eastern side of the Jordan River has been much debated. One still undeciphered inscription at Tell Deir Alla has been thought by some to be in Philistine writing, but so far this has not been proven.

The contacts of the Philistines with areas outside the coastal plain took place often through their military activities, such as in the battle on Mount Gilboa recorded in 1 Samuel 31. Sites in the Shephelah, such as Beth Shemesh, and several in the Negev, such as Tell Jemmeh, also have produced Philistine evidence.

PHILISTINE POTTERY

Of the many pottery types throughout the periods of Palestinian archaeology Philistine vessels are some of the easiest to recognize. Philistine potters employed a technique by which they covered the surface of their pottery with a white-to-gray coating called a *slip*. Over this they painted black and red figures and motifs bordered by straight or wavy lines. One common motif was a swan whose long neck and head were turned to the rear. Another motif was a swirl of concentric circles. This bichrome decoration was used on a great many single-handled jugs, medium-sized bowls, and jugs with a spout that some have taken to be beer containers.

It appears now that the decorative techniques employed by the Philistine potters represent a continuation of traditions taken with them when they left their homeland in the Aegean area. During the thirteenth century B.C.E., potters in Greece, Crete, and Cyprus were producing the finely made Mycenaean, Minoan,

Figure 8.1. Philistine jar from Gezer decorated with swans.

and Cypriot wares. These vessels contained many of the motifs of lines and circles, along with the tradition of painted surfaces, that the Philistine potters later were to adapt to their own tradition. It should be noted, however, that a minority of scholars has questioned the identification of this type of pottery with the Philistines. These researchers have raised the broader issue of whether it is possible at all to use pottery to designate particular ethnic groups such as the Philistines or (as will be seen) the Hebrews. For most Palestinian archaeologists, however, the association still holds.

THE PHILISTINES AND IRON

Since the Bible reports that at one point the Philistines had monopolized the metals market (1 Sam. 13:19), a much-discussed subject has been whether this people introduced iron workmanship into Palestine, and whether it did not at the same time also control the iron industry. It would be going too far to say that the Philistines were the sole founders of the iron industry in Palestine, since recently recovered data from the latter part of the Late Bronze Age include iron implements, and these suggest that iron-working was already known prior to the time of the Philistines. On the other hand, research has shown that Cyprus for one was a major developer of iron metallurgy, and it might be assumed that the Philistines shared in the knowledge of metal-making popular on this island of the Mediterranean. The problem is complicated by the fact that relatively few metals have come from Philistine sites in Palestine thus far excavated.

THE HEBREWS

Not only the Philistines but also the Hebrews were settling the land about 1200 B.C.E. According to many biblical scholars, this group's departure from Egypt as described in the Bible would have taken place sometime during the reign of Pharaoh Rameses II (1279–1212 B.C.E.). This would mean further that the Hebrews began to enter the land of Canaan toward the latter part of the thirteenth century B.C.E., at about the end of the Late Bronze Age in archaeological terms. The Philistines and Hebrews thus found themselves at times laying claim to the same territory, such as in the region of the Shephelah where the conflicts associated with the story of Samson occurred (Judges 13–16), and where the tribe of Dan first attempted to settle.

The Bible describes the hostility between the Philistines and Hebrews, now called Israelites, in a number of places. At the time of Samuel a major battle took place, during which the Israelites were defeated at Ebenezer near Aphek (1 Samuel 4). During Saul's kingship the Philistine army was encountered along the Esdraelon Plain, and Saul and Jonathan were killed in a battle that took place on Mount Gilboa overlooking the Esdraelon Plain (1 Samuel 31). Later the famous duel between

David and the Philistine Goliath reportedly occurred at Socoh in the Shephelah southwest of Jerusalem (1 Samuel 17).

IDENTIFYING HEBREW CULTURAL ELEMENTS

As in the case of the Philistines, a question that arises is whether it is possible to distinguish archaeological evidence that could be associated with the Hebrews. Two items in particular have been pointed to as having possible significance for identifying Israelite activity at a site or in an area.

One such item was a large storage jar with a thin, raised band on the neck or upper shoulder below the rim. Described as a

Figure 8.2. Collared-rim store jar from Taanach.

collar, this raised band gave the jar its name. Since jars of this type appeared for the first time shortly after the end of the Late Bronze Age, the interpretation has been proposed that they were introduced by the Israelites. Consequently, wherever jars of this type have been found in excavations, the issue has been raised whether we are dealing with an indicator of Israelite occupation. After about 900 B.C.E. this type of jar rim passed out of use.

Some scholars have challenged the association of the collared-rim jar with the Israelites, however. They have pointed out that the same type of jar has been found at Iron Age sites in Transjordan, and that it had a much wider dissemination. On the other hand, the fact that a much larger quantity of these storage vessels has appeared in the hill country seems significant. Jars of this type have been rare at coastal plain sites, and although examples have been found at sites such as Sahab in Transjordan, their presence there could be explained as containers in which exported goods such as olive oil were received from the hill country west of the Jordan River.

A second possible indicator of Hebrew settlement was a distinctive kind of house architecture that appeared during the early Iron Age. Many hill country sites have produced examples of this house type. These houses, whose walls were of mudbrick set on a stone foundation, had a similar pattern. Entry through a doorway led into an open court area, which also served as a place where food was prepared, since ovens (*tabuns*) were commonly found here. Around the court area were rooms, customarily three in number, so that together with the court the house came to be called a four-room house.

Several adaptations of the four-room house have been traced, but on the whole the pattern was similar. The question of whether or not these houses were used exclusively by the Israelites has been debated. Examples of a similar type of house have been found at sites such as Tawilan in Jordan, although these cases seem to be the exception rather than the rule. As in the case of identifying a certain type of pottery ethnically, some scholars have criticized the idea of associating architectural features with a particular people.

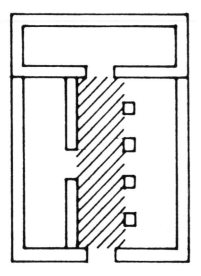

Figure 8.3. Schematic drawing of a four-room house of the Iron Age.

THE SETTLEMENT OF THE HILL COUNTRY

In addition to the collared-rim jar and the four-room house, the most recent efforts to trace evidence of the Israelites' entry into Canaan have concentrated on surveys of the hill country region. According to the Bible, it was primarily in the central hilly area of the land that the Israelites first began to settle. Thus it seemed that looking for evidence of the settlement patterns of this region might help to clarify the earliest Israelite occupation. Recent surveys have shown that many previously uninhabited sites in the hill country were first settled in the period between the twelfth and tenth centuries B.C.E. The proposal by some, then, has been that these new settlers were members of groups that eventually constituted the Israelites.

Important for these conclusions is that during the previous Late Bronze Age the hilly regions were largely ignored. The rocky soils of the hills presented difficulties for farming, in contrast to the plains where soils were richer and easier to work. Consequently, the Late Bronze occupants established their city-states mainly in these fertile plains. Megiddo in the Esdraelon Plain was one example. By the beginning of the twelfth century B.C.E., however, the new settlements were beginning to appear in the hill country. Since these hill country sites for the most part have given no indication of having been used by local Canaanites or other indigenous groups, the conclusion seems compelling that the remains at these sites were those of the early Israelites making their entrance into the land.

THE BIBLE'S MIXED PICTURE

Before turning to the archaeological data, it is necessary to look at the way the Bible depicts how the Israelites came into possession of the land. As many biblical commentators have pointed out, in the two biblical books that deal with these matters, the books of Joshua and Judges, we find two quite different, even contradictory, descriptions of the events connected with the entry into Palestine.

As the Book of Joshua presents the story, the incoming Hebrews crossed the Jordan River at Adam, a point just north of Jericho. Then, after securing the city of Jericho (Joshua 6–8), they moved into the hill country to take possession of the cities of 'Ai and Bethel (Joshua 8). From there they struck out to the southwest, where they defeated a coalition of Canaanite kings, including the king of Jerusalem, following an intense battle (Joshua 9). Finally, the Israelite militia moved northward to the Galilee region, where they took on and defeated the city of Hazor (Joshua 11). This description in the Book of Joshua, then, assumes that the Hebrews took control of many parts of the land by force, and that, following their extended series of victories, the conquered territories were parceled out as inheritances to the different participating tribal groups (Joshua 13–21).

A number of clues in the Book of Joshua itself, however, raise questions about whether the events took place in the way they are described in Joshua 1–11. First, several compositional features suggest that the Book of Joshua was produced at a time considerably after the events it was trying to describe. The tribal boundary lists in Joshua 13–21, for example, point to a period when the political system in Israel had become centralized. This would suggest a time period sometime after the monarchy had been established. The city list in Joshua 15:20–63 also reflects a later time by which many of the towns noted had been built up.

Although older accounts were used in the composition of the Book of Joshua, much of this material, too, was reorganized for the purposes of the later composition.

Observations such as these have led biblical scholars to conclude that the Book of Joshua in its final form appeared only a decade or two before the Babylonian destruction of Judah in 586 B.C.E. The composers of the Book of Joshua had a theological intent when describing the history of Israel, to stress that the land was presented as a gift through a series of wondrously won wars. In this way they could also explain in a prophetic way that the impending loss of the land by Babylonian invasion would come as a result of unfaithfulness. Although this theological motive had its own justification, scholars have questioned whether the conquest of Canaan ever occurred as it was described in this book.

What adds weight to such a conclusion is that in the Book of Judges a very different picture of the settlement of the Hebrews was portrayed. According to the Book of Judges, the Canaanites held on to their main cities and territories, and the Israelites were not able to drive them out at once (Judg. 1:19–36). Thus in this view the occupation of the land took place more deliberately over a longer period of time. Not until the tenth century, at the time of David, were many parts of the country brought under Israelite control, and it was only David who finally broke the power of the Philistines as well (2 Sam. 8:1).

We can conclude from this that the Bible's own accounts seem to indicate a more gradual possession of the land by the Hebrews. The archaeological picture, as it will be looked at momentarily, also seems to support a more extended period of Hebrew settlement in the land. This need not mean that there were no conflicts, even some of the type described in the Book of Joshua. Hostilities with the Philistines no doubt occurred much as the Bible describes them. And it may well be that skirmishes with local Canaanite towns and cities took place. But the notion of a lightning attack of entering Hebrews against the Canaanite city-states appears to be warranted neither from a biblical nor an archaeological perspective.

THE DESTRUCTION OF LATE BRONZE AGE CITIES

Now we must turn to some of the main archaeological data bearing on this problem. Particularly important is the archaeology of the end of the Late Bronze Age, together with evidence for what followed in the first phase of the Iron Age. Excavations have shown that several Late Bronze Age cities such as Bethel, Tell Beit Mirsim, Lachish, and Hazor were destroyed at the end of the period. For some archaeologists this has suggested that these destructions were indeed caused by the incoming Hebrews, and this has led them to place more credence in the Book of Joshua's account. As an example, at Hazor the conclusion was advanced that the final city of the Late Bronze Age was destroyed, only to be followed by a succeeding simpler Iron I settlement built over the Late Bronze ruins. Since Hazor was one of the cities the Book of Joshua attributed to Joshua's conquest (Josh. 11:10–15), it seemed a simple matter to associate the Late Bronze Age destruction with the biblical account.

Standing by itself the Hazor evidence would seem to be convincing. When it is looked at in relation to the entire chain of cities said to have been conquered in the Book of Joshua, however, the conclusion loses much of its force. A major problem at all of the sites, including Hazor, is whether the several destructions of Late Bronze Age cities in Palestine all belonged to the same events. As has been seen, Palestine was in a state of unrest generally toward the end of the thirteenth and the beginning of the twelfth centuries. Not only were the Hebrews settling the land, but the arrival of the Philistines was occurring at approximately the same time. Thus the destructions of Late Bronze Age cities such as Lachish or Tell Beit Mirsim could have been carried out by Philistines as well as the Hebrews. Since both sites were closer to the Philistine domain, their conquest by the former would seem more likely.

In addition, the excavations at key Late Bronze Age sites such as Taanach, Megiddo, and Beth-shean also indicated destructions sometime in the thirteenth century B.C.E., but these destructions were related to other causes, such as local conflicts or hostile interference from Egypt. That in itself suggests the difficulties of connecting certain destructions with the Israelites. Both Jericho and 'Ai, which figure prominently in the conquest narrative of the Book of Joshua, have problems as far as relating the archaeology of the end of the Late Bronze Age to the conquest account is concerned. Excavations at Jericho lacked evidence that could be connected with an invasion by Joshua, and the work done at 'Ai showed that there was no Late Bronze Age city at this site to begin with.

On the other hand, when the archaeological data are put together with the Book of Judges's perspective of a more extended period of Hebrew settlement in the land, a clearer picture emerges. We have already noted that surveys in the hill country have discovered that a sizable number of new settlements were established in the highlands during the first part of the Iron Age, pointing to a new settlement pattern that may be possible to connect with the Israelites. As the Book of Judges presents it, then, the previously large Canaanite cities in the fertile plains only later fell into the hands of the Hebrew people.

CHOOSING AMONG ALTERNATIVE VIEWS

It must be stressed that neither of the two interpretations presented above is beyond argument. The debates about the Israelite settlement will continue in the future, and both archaeology and further biblical investigation will contribute to the discussion. To make matters more complex, one or two other models have been proposed for explaining the settlement of the Israelites.

One of these models has suggested that when we encounter the Hebrews for the first time in the Bible, we meet them as part of a group of oppressed classes resisting the dominant political system of the region. The first such system from which the Hebrews experienced liberation was Egypt, but they soon ran up against a similar situation in the case of the powerful city-states of Canaan. The Hebrew struggle was consequently not so much a conquest of the land as a response to suppression. This interpretation thus falls somewhere between that of conquest and gradual settlement models. The problem with it archaeologically, in addition to the fact that it seems to impose a modern perspective on an ancient society, is that it is difficult to determine how archaeological data could be interpreted as evidence of local resistance to a state. On the other hand, such an interpretation may best explain the account of Deborah's leadership of the tribes against a joint force of Philistines and Canaanites near Taanach (Judg. 5:19).

The most promising course, then, may be to see the Hebrew settlement as one taking place gradually over a period of time, and accompanied occasionally by military skirmishes. In any case, recent evidence from the hill country is helping archaeologists to reconstruct some features of early Israelite life in the villages of this region. The villages were not large, and none of them seems to have been walled. The lack of larger public structures indicates that the communities who lived here were mostly egalitarian. Life was challenging, since cultivating the rocky slopes was not easy. At the heart of the community was the family, which shared different demands of daily subsistence. Women, too, participated in responding to these challenges, and there is good reason to believe that the relationships between women and men in the family were complementary, in comparison to urban settlements where roles were more defined and where men assumed leadership positions not usually participated in by women. Some aspects about the religious life of the Israelites in the hill country have also been recovered, and data such as these have begun to contribute new insights into the early history of Israel's religion. The discussions about this material are lively ones at present, revolving around the problem of how the early Israelites were related to the Canaanites.

9

The Birth of the Israelite Nation

At the end of the eleventh century a young shepherd named David left his home in Bethlehem to become leader over his country. Under David the Hebrew tribes were brought together into a new unity that was soon to enlarge into a nation-state with David as ruler. The events surrounding the formation of this state have left many marks on the archaeological remains of Palestine during this period.

THE BIBLE'S DESCRIPTION OF DAVID

The Bible records David's career with unusual realism and honesty. The "Court History of David" (2 Samuel 9–21, 1 Kings 1–2) depicts his important role in bringing about the national unity called Israel. By David's time the hill country settlers had already become the main occupants of the previously Canaanite cities, and thus David's mercenary military force was successful in assuring broad control over much of the country. His army also brought the kingdoms of Transjordan and territories as far away as Syria under Israelite hegemony. David's son Solomon inherited this emerging Israelite state, focusing his energies on internal construction projects such as the erection of the Jerusalem temple. Under both kings the evolving state brought about radical changes in the socioeconomic, political, and religious life of the people.

THE ARCHAEOLOGY OF IRON AGE I

The transition from a looser organization of villages and tribes to a state is documented in the biblical writings. In recent years researchers have become interested how the archaeological material from this period might shed light on these shifts in the political and social structure of the united monarchy. In what

116

follows we shall examine some aspects of the archaeology of the late eleventh and tenth centuries B.C.E., a time known to archaeologists as the latter part of Iron I.

In order to comprehend the problem of late eleventh- and tenth-century archaeology, it is necessary to consider a model advanced by the late W. F. Albright, the renowned American scholar of Near Eastern studies, who pioneered many of the approaches still used in Palestinian archaeology. On the basis of his excavations at a mound near Hebron called Tell Beit Mirsim, Albright proposed a three-stage development in the culture of the twelfth to the tenth centuries B.C.E. In the first stage, during much of the twelfth century, he noted a pre-Philistine culture. This culture produced pottery that continued some of the features of Late Bronze Age Canaan, but it also introduced new elements of its own, some of which Albright identified with the early Israelites.

Toward the end of the twelfth century there began a second stage during which Philistine pottery predominated. This stage lasted until the end of the eleventh century, and although it was concentrated along the southwest coastal plain, evidence of it was found at many inland sites as well. Finally, during the third and final stage, a new type of pottery began to appear. This pottery was described as red-slipped with hand-burnishing. The first appearance of pottery of this type occurred toward the end of the eleventh century.

Critics have held that this three-stage model is too schematic and that it did not take into account other types of cultural remains that more recent excavations have shown existed during the same period. Nonetheless, it is common today in thinking of Iron I to understand the period as dividing basically into three phases.

In the previous chapter we saw how some researchers have held that the first phase of this period reflected the emergence of Israelite tribes in Palestine, especially in the hill country where

Iron IA	1200–1125 B.C.E.
Iron IB	1125–1020 B.C.E.
Iron IC	1020–926 B.C.E.

many new sites were established. During the second phase, as Philistine wares appeared, pointing to the activities of this recently arrived people, the Israelite settlements also continued to grow. New establishments like the large farmstead at Isbet Sartah east of Tel Aviv have been interpreted as Israelite.

In this chapter we are concerned with the third phase, since this phase is associated with the changes introduced by the new state under the leadership of David. Albright was one of the first to call attention to the probable connection between the red-slipped burnished wares characteristic of this third phase and the emerging kingdom of Israel under David.

A NEW POTTERY

The new pottery tradition that began in the late eleventh century not only introduced a new repertory of forms, it also employed a technique of decoration using a red or brownish-red slip on the surface of many pottery vessels. The slip was made from iron-rich clays mixed with water; when applied, it produced a fine red or brown-to-red surface color. Many vessels were left

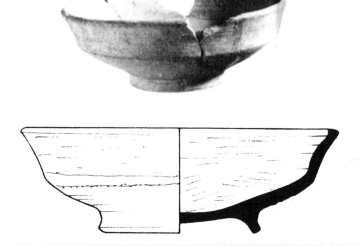

Figure 9.1. Late tenth century B.C.E. carinated bowl from Taanach.

in this state alone, and thus were slipped but not burnished. Burnishing took the decoration a step further. Using a bone or flattened stone, the potter rubbed the surface with rapid strokes, producing a glossy sheen. On many vessels of this period the direction of the burnishing is easily observed. Some vessels have straight strokes made in a vertical or horizontal direction. Others show strokes in many directions, a feature called continuous burnishing.

The application of these decorative techniques was done on bowls, jugs, juglets, smaller jars, and particularly on special objects that were made for ritual use. A popular bowl was a medium-sized dish with a low profile and a keel or carination on the shoulder. Such bowls, known as "red-slipped, burnished, carinated bowls," are a well-known diagnostic feature of tenth-century Palestine. These bowls have come to be associated with the times of Solomon since they were made in great numbers during the third quarter of the tenth century, the period of his reign. Ritual items, such as the cult stand from Taanach, were similarly treated with red slip and burnishing. This object stands approximately sixty centimeters high and is richly decorated with human and animal figures and floral designs.

THE SOCIAL SIGNIFICANCE OF RED-SLIPPED BURNISHED WARES

The red-slipped burnished ware is the cultural counterpart of the new social conditions of David's rule. It also suggests the new contacts with the world outside Palestine during this time, since the red-slipped burnished tradition apparently originated in the 'Amuq valley region of Syria. It was in this area that a related people called the Aramaeans lived, and the pottery of this type may be traceable back to them.

The Second Book of Samuel's description of David as opening up relations with the region of Aram (2 Samuel 8, 10) may help explain the influx of red-burnished red wares into Palestine at this time. Military personnel and government officials who accompanied David on his expeditions in Syria may have brought back pottery of this type. Alternatively, some potters who produced red-slipped wares may even have emigrated to Palestine.

Figure 9.2. Cult stand with mythological motifs from Taanach.

Or, it may simply have happened that potters in Palestine began to learn the technique of producing this type of pottery under influences coming from the north.

Thus the appearance of this unique pottery stimulated broader investigation of the social and political changes occurring under the united monarchy of David and Solomon. Since this type of pottery was widely made during the tenth century, it has become a key for examining the various types of settlement remains with which it was found. In other words, gates, defensive walls, houses, sanctuaries, and a variety of artifacts found together with this type of pottery have been associated with the times of either David, during the earlier stage, or Solomon.

One matter still debated is whether the red-slipped burnished pottery actually began during the reign of David, or whether it first appeared later in the tenth century, that is, during the time of Solomon. At the excavations at Taanach, a small amount of red-slipped (although not usually burnished) pottery was found in soil layers directly below those dating to the later tenth century, suggesting that this type of pottery began to be introduced during David's time. Evidence at other sites, such as 'Ain Shems, indicated a similar picture. At Gezer, however, the introduction of red-slipped burnished pottery was found first in association with the construction of the four-entryway gate at this site, and thus with the time of Solomon. In any case, although there are indications that this pottery was introduced during David's time, it is clear that its production flourished during the reign of Solomon.

ARCHAEOLOGICAL REMAINS FROM DAVID'S TIME

Several conclusions can thus be drawn from the archaeological remains dealing with David's activity. One is that some notable changes occurred at sites in the northern part of Palestine at the time David reigned from Jerusalem. The large, originally Canaanite cities in the north, such as Megiddo, Taanach, Bethshean, and Yoqneam, have all produced a similar kind of evidence of a new settlement phase occurring at this time. The new settlements were not large ones like those of the earlier Canaanite urban centers. Nonetheless, they represented serious if modest building efforts, and they clearly indicated David's interests in the northern region of the country.

The picture in the south of Palestine, where the Philistines were still a people to be reckoned with, also showed the results of David's endeavors. A key archaeological site has been Tell Qasile, located near the mouth of the Yarkon River. Excavations there have produced a remarkable structure that has been interpreted as a Philistine temple. An unusual phenomenon in the temple at Tell Qasile was that red-slipped burnished pottery appeared in one of the rooms together with Philistine vessels dating to the eleventh century. This has led excavators at Tell

Qasile to conclude that at their site the date of red-burnished pottery should be placed earlier in the eleventh century. Others have argued, however, that since temple traditions are conservative, the Philistine pottery could have been in use down to a later time. Thus, it would not follow that red-burnished wares generally should be dated by the unusual context at this site. According to the excavators this phase at Tell Qasile was destroyed by David, following which a new city was built during Solomon's reign.

Similar changes took place at two other southern sites at the end of the eleventh and beginning of the tenth centuries B.C.E. Beth Shemesh was located farther inland, and here again a city was apparently constructed under David, only to be expanded under Solomon. The case with Gezer was different. Although it too was rebuilt during the time of David, it apparently did not become an Israelite city until the time of Solomon, as also suggested by the Bible (1 Kgs. 9:16).

These features of the archaeology of the time of David illustrate some of the dynamics occurring as the new state of Israel was emerging under this king. By David's choice the city of Jerusalem also became the center from which the whole of his kingdom would be administered. In contrast to the earlier Bronze Age city-states, the establishment of one city as the capital was an innovation with important implications. The effort to centralize the affairs of government not only provided political security, it also brought economic advantages to a good number of the population. Solomon's reign developed further these dynamics of the emerging Israelite state.

ARCHAEOLOGICAL REMAINS FROM SOLOMON'S TIME

The archaeological data from Solomon's time are among the most abundant of any part of the Iron Age related to the biblical period. Probably at no time during the united or divided kingdom of Israel was so much government construction undertaken as during the reign of Solomon. This is indicated in many places in the biblical texts about Solomon, but the archaeological evidence surpasses the Bible in the broad amount of material discovered. Once again the red-slipped burnished pottery is the key, since this pottery had become widely distributed by the

> Commonly recognized as one of the great literary and histori-
> cal pieces of the Bible, 2 Samuel 9–20 together with 1 Kings
> 1–2 are referred to as "The Court History of David." This narra-
> tive traces David's foibles as well as his strengths with an hon-
> esty not often seen in ancient writing. The tense events lead-
> ing to Solomon's succession are also part of this document.

time of Solomon during the second half of the tenth century
B.C.E.

Two sites at which important building activities took place
during the reign of Solomon were Megiddo and Taanach. From
the Bible we know that these were important cities in the north
(1 Kgs. 4:12). When Megiddo was excavated by the Oriental
Institute of the University of Chicago in the 1930s, it was concluded that one of the major strata of the Iron Age belonged to
the building activities of Solomon. Although some modifications
in interpreting the stratigraphy of Megiddo have been made since
the time of the excavations, it has been shown that a combination
of two levels, now joined as Stratum VA–IVB, is to be associated
with the age of Solomon. It is this stratum that has been mainly
preserved at the site of Megiddo, and any visitor to the site today
can view the basic plan of the stratum of Solomon's time.

The construction of Megiddo seemed to follow a plan used at
several other cities during Solomon's age, such as Gezer and
Hazor. The city was surrounded by what some have argued was
a *casemate wall*—a type of defensive system consisting of two
walls built parallel to one another. In this system crosswalls were
placed between the parallel city walls, creating small rooms that
could be used as dwellings or that sometimes served for those
guarding the city. The advantage of a casemate wall was that it
secured the city more strongly than a wall consisting of a single
line. The proposal that such a wall was found at Megiddo has
been intensely debated, however. Some researchers favor the
interpretation of a casemate wall associated with the Stratum
VA–IVB city, while others doubt that such a wall was present at
all. The matter is complicated by the fact that key data bearing on this problem were removed by earlier excavators. But if

Figure 9.3. Four-entryway gate at Gezer.

Megiddo was built on the same plan as Gezer and Hazor, both of which had casemate walls along with their large gateways, the same thing might be expected there.

The modern visitor to Megiddo can view the impressive four-entryway gate of Stratum VA–IVB, since one side was well preserved. Made of impressively dressed boulders, the gate was designed with four entries, just like the outstandingly preserved gate at Gezer. Three rooms on each side of the gateway opened out to the thoroughfare of people coming and going through the gate. Each of these rooms had benching on its three sides, where people might rest or meetings might take place. Chambers such as those found in the Solomonic gateways at Megiddo and Gezer are thus good illustrations of what the phrase "justice in the gate" might mean, as found in the Bible (Amos 5:15). Since Iron Age cities had no special building for a court of judgment, those leaders in ancient Israel responsible for adjudicating legal dis-

124

putes carried this on in gate-rooms of this type. At other times in the Iron Age, however, this kind of activity would have taken place in the vicinity of the gate and not within rooms, since the latter were not always found in gates of the later phases.

The interior of the city of Megiddo had dwellings sometimes bordering on adjacent streets. There were also government buildings, such as a structure called Palace 6000. This building had apparently served for the administration of Solomon's activities in this city. Palace 6000 was a rectangular building with an open court in its center. On the north were five large rooms, while on the east and west were hallways, and on the south a hallway and a room. The southeast corner apparently had a tower. It has been suggested that this building was constructed in a style of palace building that went back to the Hittites. Since buildings of this type have been found along the Phoenician coast, and since the Bible records that Solomon made use of Phoenician builders in the construction of the temple (1 Kgs. 5:1–6), this palace may be another example of influence from the Phoenician area, although originally of Hittite inspiration. It is also a further indication of the extent of international contacts and influences during Solomon's reign.

The religious activities during the age of Solomon were also illuminated in the findings at Megiddo. A possible sanctuary or cult building, designated simply Building 2081, contained many examples of red-slipped burnished pottery. Many of these items were exquisitely made, including incense burners and cult stands. Nearby were a number of small stone altars with "horns" on their four corners. Other examples of horned altars have appeared recently at Beer-sheba (a full-sized example), Dan, and Tel Miqne. The reference to an altar with horns in the Bible (Exod. 30:2–3) apparently had to do with this basic type, although the example specified in the Book of Exodus was to be made of acacia wood and covered with gold.

A structure similar to Building 2081 at Megiddo was a building called the Cultic Structure at Taanach. Like the Megiddo example, the Taanach building also contained many unusual red-slipped burnished vessels, and three groups of sheep astragali totaling 140 altogether. A figurine mold was also uncovered, and since the large stone on the eastern side of the Cultic Structure had been carefully hewn and smoothed, it may have been an example of what the Bible calls a pillar (*mazzebah* in Hebrew). The Bible associates such pillars with the religion of the Canaanites (Deut. 12:3), but the archaeological study of raised pillars is still going on, and their various possible functions are not yet clear.

These materials from Megiddo and Taanach may, then, coincide with the Bible's later interpretation that a good deal of religious syncretism had occurred during Solomon's reign (1 Kgs. 11:1–8). This seems especially to have been the case in cities farther north, such as those in the Esdraelon Plain that were located close to the Canaanite center of Tyre along the ancient Syrian coast. Excavations in Jerusalem have also uncovered cultic material of Canaanite background dating to Solomon's time and after. The biblical account of Solomon also reports the shrines he had built for several deities on the hills of Jerusalem (1 Kgs. 11:7), although no specific data have been found bearing on this account.

THE MEGIDDO STABLES DEBATE

Before leaving Megiddo it is important to look at one building that has been a center of controversy. At the time of its excavation it was concluded that this building was a large government stable built during Solomon's time. This conclusion, especially the date assigned the structure, was apparently influenced by the Bible's account of Solomon's purchase of large numbers of horses (1 Kgs. 10:26–29). When the stratigraphic evidence for this building was restudied, however, it became clear that these stables dated to the following ninth century B.C.E. rather than to the age of Solomon. That presented no problem for interpreting the building as a stable, since during the following century in an inscription of Shalmaneser III King Ahab was reported to have brought a great number of horses and chariots to the battle against the Assyrians at Qarqar in 853 B.C.E. Thus it was simply a matter of transferring the interpretation of the building as a stable from Solomon to Ahab.

But the controversy also focused on the explanation of the building as a stable, and other interpretations of its function were proposed. A number of archaeologists have attempted to determine by means of its dimensions and organization whether the building could have been used for stabling horses. Some have argued that there was not enough room for animals to be brought in and turned around in the spaces between the pillars that were taken to be horses' stalls. Alternative explanations have consequently been attempted—such as that the building served as a storehouse, a military barrack, or even that it might have been a covered marketplace. None of these alternatives, however, seems to have convincingly supplanted the interpretation of stables.

Another site at which Solomon's building activities in north Palestine were substantial is Hazor. Located along a major route tying Egypt to Syria and Mesopotamia, Hazor had a prominent history going back to the Early Bronze Age. Solomon's advisors did not overlook the importance of this city, and thus it was rebuilt during this king's reign. The stratum associated with Solomon included a casemate wall and four-entryway gate, nearly identical in its dimensions to those at Megiddo and Gezer. Thus the archaeological remains of this city, too, have been brought into the discussion about Solomon's building activities as described in the Bible (1 Kgs. 9:16).

The south also experienced the expansion of Solomon's construction projects. Gezer was built according to a plan nearly identical to that found at Megiddo and Hazor. Excavations at Gezer have revealed the clearest example of all of a casemate wall and four-entryway gate. The red-slipped burnished pottery found with the wall and gate fixed these features firmly in the age of Solomon. Other structures inside the city showed that it was a flourishing settlement during the days of Solomon. According to the biblical account (1 Kgs. 9:16), Solomon had received the site as a dowry upon his marriage to an Egyptian pharaoh's daughter (possibly Pharaoh Siamun of the Twenty-first Dynasty).

THE ARCHAEOLOGY OF JERUSALEM IN THE TIME OF THE UNITED MONARCHY

The most important city associated in the Bible with David was Jerusalem, the city that David took from the Jebusites (2 Sam. 5:6–10). During the past hundred years, a good number of archaeologists have worked with varying results on the archaeology of Jerusalem. But one of the disappointments has been the little amount of evidence dating to the united monarchy, due in no small part to the fact that Jerusalem presents special problems for archaeological work. In contrast to many abandoned sites of antiquity, Jerusalem has continued to be occupied through the centuries, which means that areas that may contain significant information have become inaccessible because of modern occupation above them.

One area that has been more or less available for excavation, however, has been the southern slope of the city. During David's time the hilly southeastern part of the city was called the Ophel. Earlier excavations in Jerusalem had uncovered an extensive stepped stone revetment system built against the slope of the Ophel hill, and more recent excavation has clarified this impressive structure, giving it a more precise dating. The recent

Figure 9.4. Stepped revetment on the south slope of Jerusalem.

excavators concluded that the stratigraphy together with the pottery made it necessary to date the stepped structure to the tenth century. That would make the construction a feature of the city of the united monarchy, most likely begun during the reign of David.

Apparently the stepped stone construction was built to stabilize the erosion-prone south slopes of the city, above which the buildings of David's citadel could be built. Although its purpose was functional, this prominent construction feature indicates the importance the city of Jerusalem assumed in the kingdoms of David and Solomon. Nothing was too costly to prepare this city for its special role.

THE TEMPLE OF SOLOMON

Although all evidence of Solomon's temple has long ago perished, this most important structure of Jerusalem also was to play a major role in Israelite society from the time it was built to its destruction by the Babylonians. The Bible itself suggests that building the temple was not only a religious act on the part of Solomon, but that it also fit with his political aspirations, as the related account of the construction of his nearby palace shows (1 Kgs. 7:1–12). Since Solomon sought the help of Phoenician builders to construct the temple (1 Kgs. 5:18), it is understandable that broader Near Eastern motifs would appear in the art and architecture of this building.

Studied archaeologically, the temple of Solomon was built on a plan similar to Bronze and Iron Age temples known from excavations in Syria. This plan consisted of a simple oblong building divided into three parts. The Jerusalem temple was beautifully decorated, especially on its interior. Most important, its impressive exterior and its location on the most prominent site of Jerusalem served as a point of integration for the united kingdom. Much later, Jerusalem priests would seriously emphasize the unification of religious life in the temple (Deuteronomy 12), but undoubtedly already in this early period, as the new state was getting underway, this was one of the most important intentions in the construction of the building. The temple would take its place as the most renowned symbol of the golden age of the united kingdom.

10

The Growth and Decline of the Divided States

In the aftermath of the days of David and Solomon the united kingdom of Israel went through a turbulent period. Shortly after Solomon's death the country was raided by the Egyptian pharaoh Shishak I (1 Kgs. 14:25–26). Dissension also arose over the economic policies of Solomon's son, Rehoboam, who was forced to tax the populace of the north more heavily to keep the state he had inherited going. As these pressures mounted, the solidarity of the single nation fell apart. The north and south regions of the country split into two kingdoms. This schism ruined what many had hoped would follow after a glorious beginning.

Yet these events did not prevent the separated kingdoms from developing their own wealth. The cultivation of foreign relations with Mesopotamia and Egypt during the ninth to the sixth centuries helped foster a new prosperity. In the end, however, irreversible decline set in in both Israel and Judah. The Bible records a political and social deterioration that began in the ninth century. The warnings of the biblical prophets were also a touchstone of deep-seated social problems in both states. The achievements and uncertainties of this period can be seen in the archaeological data of Iron II.

A TIME OF PROSPERITY

For some in the kingdoms of Israel the ninth to seventh centuries were a time of prosperity. Both kingdoms profited from the idea of a centralized government that was a legacy of the days of David and Solomon. The economies of both regions were diverse enough to stimulate growth. Surpluses in goods production contributed to a flourishing system of exchange. Excavations of olive presses at hill country sites such as Shechem in north Israel showed that olive oil was a major product that could be exported to other areas. Wheat and barley were plentiful and were also important commodities for exchange. Inscribed weights found at Iron II sites give us a glimpse into the daily sales of foodstuffs and other items.

A nuclear family of the time consisted of four or five persons, but the number was often larger when extended family members were included. Houses customarily had at least three rooms on a lower level, and additional rooms on an upper level. Family members could also sleep on flat roofs during warmer months. Most families cared for livestock, such as large cattle or sheep and goats, and these were kept in stalls also in the lower levels of the dwellings. Houses were clustered in villages, towns, or cities, and these settlements, in turn, were surrounded by open areas of cultivation, broken down into family plots.

THE ISRAELITE STATES AND THE NEAR EASTERN EMPIRES

During the ninth and seventh centuries B.C.E. the two Israelite states were drawn into international relations as never before. This had its positive side in stimulating the development of resources, but a price was also paid for such outside contacts. Beginning in the ninth century the Israelite states became participants, often unwillingly, in the designs of the new empire system. Hints of such political involvement could be seen at the time of David and Solomon, but the full entry into internationalism would not take place until the time of the divided monarchy of Israel. During the divided kingdom period, the powerful states of Assyria and Babylon emerged in Mesopotamia, only to be followed by the Persian, Greek, and Roman empires.

The policy of the first millennium Mesopotamian empires was to make frequent military expeditions to Palestine to maintain

Iron IIA	926–814 B.C.E.
Iron IIB	814–721 B.C.E.
Iron IIC	721–586 B.C.E.

control over the region. Sometimes this resulted in actual conquest, at other times in threatened attacks, with the result that treaty and payoff arrangements had to be made. Imperial records dating from the eighth and seventh centuries refer to the "taxes" that lesser kingdoms were compelled to pay in order to maintain a safe relationship with the dominant powers. The Bible has a number of references to such events (2 Kgs. 15:19, 2 Kgs. 17:3–4). If the smaller powers refused to make their payments, or worse, if they rebelled, they could be punished, as happened in the case of Sennacherib's invasion of Judah in 701 B.C.E. (2 Kgs. 18:13–16). The eighth- and seventh-century Israelite prophets delivered oracles of advice and warning about these events.

In such a threatening political environment it became necessary for cities in Palestine to protect themselves. In contrast to the Iron I period, when the Israelite villages were more or less isolated in the hill country, the Iron II towns were subject to pressures from the large powers. The loss of unity between the northern and southern kingdoms did not help the situation and, if anything, became an additional burden to the peoples of both states. It is understandable that the prophets would view the division of the kingdom as a deeply sad event in the history of the Israelite people (Jer. 23:13–14).

DEFENSE NETWORKS OF THE NEW CITIES

The threats that these two states became to each other and their fears of outside intrusion explain the expanded defensive structures found in many cities of the period. In both kingdoms, cities were constructed with new defense systems. One of the places where this was first noted was at Tell en-Nasbeh north of Jerusalem. This site was located along one of the main roadways passing from Jerusalem to the northern part of the country. It was consequently an important site, its large city wall and gateway being built to make it impervious to attack. When Tell en-Nasbeh was excavated, the excavators proposed that its defensive system must have had something to do with the political situation of the divided kingdom of Israel. They pointed to the unique orientation of the gateway, for example, that would have forced anyone entering the city to turn toward the left, thus exposing their strong side on the right. It was believed that this pattern in gate construction was purposely introduced as a response to the military threats of the time.

Whether such an explanation of the Tell en-Nasbeh gate construction is valid or not, the excavators were apparently right in assuming that much of the planning of cities during this period was related to external conditions. Since the time of the excavation of Tell en-Nasbeh, a large number of additional Iron II cities have been excavated, and many of these, too, had impressive defense systems. In the northern part of Israel the Iron II city of Dan was entered by means of a well-built gate with several entries.

Two other northern cities that were important centers of influence were Hazor and Samaria. Like Megiddo and Taanach, Hazor was reconstructed after what must have been a serious attack against this city by Shishak I. Its defensive system was rebuilt during the ninth and eighth centuries, enclosing a city that also had a good number of four-room houses. Like other cities in the north, Hazor fell to the Assyrians in 721 B.C.E., and thereafter its importance declined. Even more than Hazor, Samaria came to represent the focus of northern Israelite power. This site was first turned into a fortified city during the ninth century under Omri and Ahab, who established it as the capital of the northern kingdom. Excavations of the royal palace at Samaria uncovered examples of masonry, demonstrating the wealth of the city in the ninth and eighth centuries. The carved ivory found within the royal palace is some of the finest ever discovered in ancient Palestine.

The Second Book of Kings contains a running account of the kings of north Israel and Judah, along with a number of events that occurred in each king's reign. Second Kings 1–17 record the history of the two kingdoms up to the invasion of north Israel by the Assyrians in 721 B.C.E., while 2 Kings 18–25 continues the story of Judah to the fall of Jerusalem under the Babylonians in 586 B.C.E. The eighth and seventh centuries were the centuries of the great prophets Amos, Hosea, Isaiah, and Jeremiah.

The defenses at Megiddo were also reconstructed during the ninth and eighth centuries. Following what must have been Shishak's attack against Megiddo in approximately 920 B.C.E., the city's gate and wall were rebuilt nearly to the strength of the preceding period of Solomon. Megiddo too was to suffer attack during the Assyrian conquest of north Israel.

THE IRON II CITIES OF JUDAH

In the south, the kingdom of Judah also experienced growth, despite recurrent tensions stemming from international involvements. One of the results of recent archaeology in the city of Jerusalem has been to show how the capital city was extended and refortified during the reign of Hezekiah. Excavations determined that Hezekiah's city incorporated the large area of Mount Zion west of the earlier Iron Age city, making Jerusalem ten times larger than any other city in Judah.

During Hezekiah's reign Jerusalem also came to be enclosed by a seven-meter-wide wall made of large undressed stones. On the eastern side of the city stood the glorious temple of Solomon. Some of the late-seventh-century houses discovered in recent excavation, such as the "burnt house," demonstrated the impressive construction used in domestic structures. Jerusalem of the eighth and seventh centuries was an impressive city, and its occupants enjoyed a high standard of living.

Access to Jerusalem's most important water supply, the Gihon spring at the southeastern end of the city, was assured by means of an underground connection called the Siloam tunnel. This important engineering feat meant that the city's water supply could now be safely contained within the city, and the populace of Jerusalem would not be cut off from it in the event of attack. The dedicatory inscription of this tunnel, found long ago and now housed in a museum in Istanbul, recorded that the tunnel was constructed during the days of Hezekiah.

Cities of considerable size during the eighth and seventh centuries were also found in the Shephelah, the coastal region, and the Negev. One example was Lachish, excavated earlier by a British and more recently by an Israeli team. That Lachish was a wealthy city during the Iron II period was evident from its massive gate and its fortification system comprised of two par-

Figure 10.1. The Siloam tunnel from King Hezekiah's time.

allel city walls encircling the city. On the interior were well-built houses. The city's importance politically was indicated by the large government buildings dating to the eighth century.

As one of the larger cities in the country during Iron II, Lachish was naturally a site marked for attack by an invading group. Such was the case when in 701 B.C.E. the Assyrian armies of Sennacherib laid siege to the city. This event is recorded in the Bible (2 Kgs. 18:13–18), and it was celebrated by the Assyrians on a series of immense wall reliefs discovered in the royal palace at Nineveh depicting "the siege of Lachish." Sennacherib also gave his own account of these events in his annals.

The recent excavations at Lachish have underscored the seriousness of the attack against this city, events that occurred during the time of Hezekiah and the prophet Isaiah. Ironically, it was also at Lachish at a later time in 586 B.C.E. that a further destruction by invasion occurred, this time by the Babylonians. In connection with these later events a group of ostraca found

Figure 10.2. Reconstruction of Sennacherib's siege of Lachish, based on reliefs from Nineveh.

in one of the guard rooms of the gate gave warning of the approaching Babylonian armies that would soon overrun the city. Thus it is in connection with Lachish that we have some of the best written information regarding the invasions of two different armies from Mesopotamia at two different times, which affected not only this city but also the whole country of Judah.

From archaeology we know that the southern kingdom of Judah had many other cities that were fortified during the ninth and to the seventh centuries. Although Gezer was not as impressive during these centuries as it had been during the tenth, it still maintained an important place along the lower end of the Shephelah. On the other hand, a good number of Iron II cities in the Negev indicate the importance of this region in the network of fortified cities of Judah. One of the most impressive was the later city of Arad, the city associated by the Bible with the attempted entry of the Israelites into the land of Canaan during their desert wanderings (Num. 21:1). Although excavations at Arad produced few Iron Age remains prior to the tenth century, which is a problem for the biblical account, the site became a bastion in southern Judah during the Iron II period. On its high hill stood the Judean fortress that has been impressively reconstructed following the excavations. Its strategic location provided special protection in the event of military activity (from Egypt, in particular).

An important building at Arad, its Iron Age sanctuary, has been much studied by researchers since its basic form has been taken to parallel the plan of the Jerusalem temple as spelled out in 1 Kings 6. The Arad sanctuary consisted of an elongated structure, with what some have argued was a special room, a "holy of holies," at its far end. Two additional rooms in front of this room were then thought to conform to the tripartite plan of the Jerusalem temple described in the Bible. The problem of whether or not the Arad sanctuary corresponds architecturally to the Jerusalem temple is still very much debated, however.

Some forty kilometers west of Arad lay the city of Beer-sheba, the most prominent Iron II city in the Negev. From the tenth century to the end of the Iron Age, Beer-sheba stood as perhaps the most strongly fortified city in the southland of Judah. Excavations at this site produced one of the most complete plans of an Iron Age II city yet uncovered. The city was walled and, as in the case of other Iron II cities, the approach to the interior was through a gate with three entries. Immediately in front of the interior of the gate was an open area that served as a meeting place for public activity or as a market area. Just beyond the gate were several major government storage buildings, in front of which a circular street proceeded around the entire interior of the city. Several other streets radiated from this circular thoroughfare, and domestic structures and other buildings were located in relation to the streets.

Beer-sheba was thus a further example of a fortified city during Iron II, corresponding to Lachish and the fortress at Arad. Yet other sites in the Negev were also fortified during this period. Examples were Tel Masos, Aro'er, and Tel Ira, as well as Kadesh Barnea farther to the south. Thus a considerable spread of settlements as well as accompanying political control was cultivated by the Judean state in this southern part of the country during the eighth century. This was necessary because in this area the threat of attack might come from Egypt, which continued to be a power until the time of the Babylonian destruction, or from the Edomites, a desert people often infringing upon the territory of southern Judah, or from the local desert tribes who might sometimes attempt raids against these settlements.

CHANGES IN THE POTTERY TRADITIONS

The traditions of pottery production reflected some of these political and social conditions of the period. In the early ninth century, despite the political divisions beginning to emerge, pottery types remained similar in the northern and southern parts of the country. Red-slipped burnishing continued in vogue, used especially on bowls of various sizes and shapes. An innovation was the introduction early in the ninth century of the fast pottery wheel. Pottery could more readily be mass-produced, in both areas of the country. The ceramic traditions thus indicate that, although the north and south regions were now set against one another politically, a good deal of cultural interchange continued during the early part of the ninth century.

By the late ninth and the following century the two regions became more isolated from one another. This can be observed in the way vessels such as jugs and jars were increasingly profiled in different manners at northern and southern sites. At the same time, however, the so-called Israelite water decanter was found in both the north and south, with variations in the rims of these vessels according to one region or the other.

During the latter quarter of the eighth century the invasion of the northern kingdom by the Assyrians resulted in the isolation of north Israel from Judah. The assault of the Assyrians on the north has been traced in the archaeological remains at sites such as Samaria, Shechem, and Hazor. In the aftermath of this invasion, pottery-making began to incorporate foreign types such as a type of ceramic called "Assyrian palace ware." A prime example of this palace ware was a bowl made from fine clay, displaying curved sidewalls and decorated with a burnished red slip. Black wares were also present in this group.

Recently it has also been shown that the decoration of some bowls with small wedge-shaped indentations on the interior also goes back to Assyrian influence during this period. Although the cuneiform-like patterns do not suggest intelligible writing, they probably reflected the use of a stylus similar to that used in the writing of cuneiform. Since such wedge-shaped writing was done in Mesopotamia and not in Palestine, it is understandable that this type of decoration began to manifest itself only after the Assyrians had settled some of their own people in the northern areas of Palestine.

OSTRACA AND STAMPED JAR HANDLES

The economic, social, and political situations in the two parts of the country are illuminated by means of a group of ostraca found at the northern capital of Samaria, and various stamped jar handles from sites in the south. Both the ostraca (potsherds with writing on them) and stamped jar handles provide important information regarding the administration of the country during the period of the divided monarchy.

The Samaria ostraca were found in a building on the eastern side of the court of the great palace excavated at Samaria. The original construction of the palace took place during the time of Ahab, but the palace continued in use much later. The sixty-three ostraca found in the debris of the building have been dated to the century following Ahab, the eighth century B.C.E. Each ostracon usually contained a brief account of a shipment of wine or oil from one party to another. Since these items were found in the precincts of the royal palace, they apparently represent government documents of some type.

A number of interpretations of the social meaning of the Samaria ostraca have been proposed by scholars. One view is that the ostraca were receipts that accompanied shipment of oil or wine to the royal depository. This would possibly indicate some form of taxation or, if the localities from which the items came were royal estates, income for the treasury. The opposite interpretation has also been proposed, that the ostraca represented accounts of shipments from the palace storehouses to outlying localities. Regardless of which interpretation is correct, all would

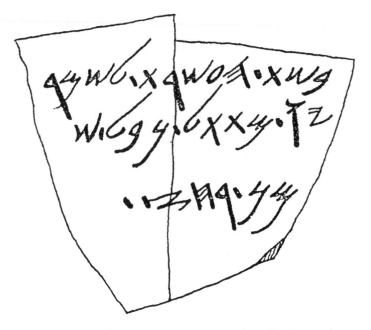

Figure 10.3. Drawing of a Samaria ostracon, reading "in the tenth year, to Shemaryahu from Tetel, a jar of fine oil."

agree that these documents deal in some way with the political and economic situation in the northern kingdom.

For approximately two centuries, then, the northern kingdom of Israel experienced a time of economic growth. Agricultural productivity was at a high level, and the upper classes in particular, as well as those in the court, benefited from these developments. The social situation behind the Samaria ostraca might suggest that wherever possible the palace attempted to take over lands as government properties. Since farmlands held previously by one family were often subdivided among sons following the death of the father, ownership was reduced to smaller plots, making these holdings perhaps more vulnerable to state expropriation. It was in the context of these developing tensions that the prophets of the eighth century rose to challenge the economic inequities in such a system, as the earlier account of Ahab's ploy to take land from Naboth, condemned by the prophet Elijah, shows (1 Kings 21).

The second group, that of storage jars with stamped jar handles, has come to light at various sites in the southern kingdom of Judah. Examples found at Lachish have established their date to the latter part of the eighth century, quite probably during the time of Hezekiah. Their significance for Judah was apparently similar to that of the ostraca for northern Israel. That is, the jars contained shipments of a commodity, most likely wine, from government production centers to outlying cities. The cities where the wine was produced were named on the stamp impressions as Hebron, Socoh, Ziph, and an unknown one spelled in Hebrew *mmsht*. Because of their strategic locations, the cities named on these stamps seem also to have played an important role in Hezekiah's efforts to ward off an attack by the Assyrians under Sennacherib (2 Kgs. 18:13–37).

THE IRON II CITIES OF TRANSJORDAN

Recent excavations in Jordan have brought radical changes to the understanding of this important region. The fallacy that Jordan was essentially an open country occupied primarily by nomadic groups during the Middle and Late Bronze ages, and even to some degree during Iron I, has been given up. It seems apparent now that this misconception arose largely as a result of the small amount of work that had been done in Jordan until the last several decades. More evidence of settlement during the Middle Bronze Age has been appearing, although this was not by any means dense occupation. During the Late Bronze Age the country witnessed the establishment of a good number of new settlements, as is increasingly clear. And Iron I data in greater amounts than previously available have come to light, changing also the perception of this period.

If the area east of the Jordan River is compared with that west of the river, a similar pattern emerges during the Iron I and II periods. In Jordan a large concentration of Iron Age sites was found in the area north of the Wadi Mojib (Nahal Arnon), well up to today's northern border. On the other hand, the number of Iron Age sites south of Wadi Mojib was found to thin out. This parallels almost exactly the situation west of the Jordan

River, where the southern extent of Iron Age sites is along a line not far from Beer-sheba in the Negev. Climatic and morphological conditions clearly affected the outer limits of Iron Age settlement on both sides of the river.

From both archaeology and literary sources, including the Bible, we know that one of the main roads leading northward to Syria and Mesopotamia ran along the east side of the Dead Sea. Known as the King's Highway (Num. 20:17), this roadway attracted significant settlement along it. Thus a clustering of Iron Age sites was located along or within close range of this major artery. Tell Dhiban, known in the Bible as Dibon (Num. 21:30), was one of these. Dibon was a walled Iron Age site that served as the capital of the kingdom of Moab. Excavations at Tell Dhiban uncovered evidence of a city lasting from the ninth century B.C.E. to the Babylonian period.

North of Dibon is Tell Hesban, where excavations found remains of settlement through both phases of the Iron Age. Attempts have been made to connect Tell Hesban with biblical Heshbon known from the account of the early Israelite wanderings through the land of Moab (Num. 21:27–28). The correspondence between the ancient name and that of the modern tell would suggest an identification. Results of the excavations have made this identification difficult, however, since no Late Bronze remains were discovered and the Iron I evidence was limited.

Other sites from the same general area are Buseireh, probably to be identified with biblical Bosra, Sahab, Tell Umeiri and Tell Safut. Each of these settlements provided further evidence of the construction of Iron Age towns, often with walls. Town and even city construction took place in Jordan during the Iron Age as it did west of the river.

Recent research devoted to the Iron Age in Jordan has focused on some of the differences between the cultures east and west of the Jordan River. Such efforts have identified pottery and other objects that can more specifically be attributed to the Moabite, Ammonite, or Edomite cultures, in contrast to those of Israel or Judah west of the Jordan River. At the same time, there were frequent contacts between the cultures of these adjacent regions, and consequently the Iron Age artifacts on either side of the river

Figure 10.4. Fortifications and a large Iron II public building at Tell Umeiri.

also have similarities. Studies have also been made of the Ammonite language in particular, and although this language was a close cousin to Hebrew, it had its differences.

Farther north in Jordan the differences in cultural features become more pronounced from those in the south or those west of the Jordan River. A case in point was the cultural material from Tell er-Rumeith, that has been identified with biblical Ramoth-Gilead. Since Tell er-Rumeith was located on the border between Jordan and Syria, the pottery demonstrates many relations to Syrian types rather than to those of Palestine.

From the ninth to the end of the seventh and beginning of the sixth centuries, then, Palestine witnessed a period of local development that allowed a number of regional kingdoms to develop on both sides of the Jordan River. Although the kingdoms of Israel and Judah made attempts at times to expand their influence into the adjacent regions, for the greater part of

143

these centuries these local kingdoms lived in less ambitious contacts with one another. During these times some exchange of goods took place, and there was a certain amount of cross-fertilization among them.

THE END OF JUDAH AND THE CLOSE OF THE IRON AGE

By the latter half of the seventh century the kingdom of Judah had spent much of its wealth. The notable expansion of the city of Jerusalem under Hezekiah may indicate that the population grew in other parts of the kingdom as well. Demographic problems, coupled with overplanted fields and a lessening supply of water, could then have severely weakened the infrastructure of the kingdom. Jeremiah's description (Jeremiah 14) of drought, and lack of food and water, paints a vivid picture of the weakened internal conditions that had developed by the last half of the seventh century.

Then with the invasion of the Babylonian military into the area, first in 598 B.C.E., and again in 586 B.C.E., the picture changed radically. With the Babylonians came the beginning of a succession of empires into the region. As the Iron Age ended, so did a significant time in the history of ancient Palestine. The archaeological picture of Iron II helps us reconstruct the unique economic and social system in Judah prior to the Babylonian destruction, and thus to preserve information on a Palestine that would thereafter be set in wholly new directions as it became a pawn in the hands of the empires.

11
Persians, Greeks, and Jewish Revolt

The Babylonians made several assaults against the kingdom of Judah before destroying it in 586 B.C.E. In a final invasion they attacked Jerusalem, ravaging its temple, houses, and city wall. Other cities, such as Lachish, were subsequently assailed. Then, in a mop-up operation, the invaders deported the Judean community's leaders as an assurance against future resistance. Many of the deportees eventually prospered in Babylon, while back in Palestine things were in shambles. For seventy years (in Jeremiah's rounded number; Jer. 25:11–12) it seemed that the homeland had reverted to a desert waste. Judeans expressed their dismay over the desolation through such prayers as those found in the Book of Lamentations.

But the balance of power would change once more. The Persians brought the empire of Babylon to an end in 539 B.C.E., substituting for the often-harsh Babylonian practice a very different approach. The prophetic books of Haggai and Zechariah suggest that on the whole the Persians encouraged their subjects to carry on projects of reconstruction and development. The more liberal spirit of this period can also be seen in the books of Ezra and Nehemiah, where an edict attributed to Cyrus allowed the exiles to return to Jerusalem to rebuild their temple (Ezra 1:2–4, 5:13).

ARCHAEOLOGICAL SITES OF THE PERSIAN PERIOD

Archaeology has shed new light in recent years on the occupation of the country by this people from the highlands of Iran. Records found in Persia itself show that Palestine became part of the region the Persians termed "Beyond the River." As a method of controlling the provinces or satrapies of their vast empire, the Persians placed governors called *satraps* over them.

145

One such governor was the much-hated Sanballat (Neh. 2:10), who obstructed the work of Nehemiah and his fellow laborers as they attempted to rebuild Jerusalem's walls.

This policy of government administration according to provinces has become clearer through recent archaeological work in different parts of Palestine where concentrations of Persian sites have been found. The locations of these sites and the patterns found in their remains show that many of them were administrative centers within the Persian satrap system. Local people often were appointed to serve in these governmental centers, which also played a role in a defense system in the event that powers (for example, Egypt) decided to make moves into the area. Such Persian settlements were established along the Mediterranean coast, while others have been excavated in the hill country of Palestine, and in the Jordan valley.

Three important sites along the Mediterranean coast where Persian remains have been found are Dor, Ashdod, and Ashkelon. Each of these sites had much earlier been occupied by the Philistines, but by the Persian period much of that past had been forgotten. Now these old Philistine sites were incorporated into the Persian organization of the country. In a number of areas excavated at Dor, Persian occupation was found in the form of building remains that were often fragmentary since Dor was soon succeeded by a larger Hellenistic city whose foundations were set into the Persian remains. Another old Philistine city, Ashdod, also had substantial Persian remains, including a large public building that again probably reflected the administrative role of this settlement.

The recent work at Ashkelon has thrown light on daily life during this period. Ashkelon does not seem to have been a typical Persian city, but its unique character is instructive for the

Neo-Babylonian	586–539 B.C.E.
Persian I	539–450 B.C.E.
Persian II	450–332 B.C.E.
Early Hellenistic	332–198 B.C.E.
Late Hellenistic	198–63 B.C.E.

The Persian conquerors of ancient Palestine introduced a new system of government control in the land. Characteristic of this period were small sites where local government buildings were constructed. That Palestine was now just one small segment in the far-flung empire of the Persians is apparent from the archaeological remains. Biblical books dealing with the Persian Period are the Books of Ezra and Nehemiah.

variety of peoples during the period. The Persian period population at Ashkelon consisted of an ethnic mix of Greeks, Phoenicians, Jews, and probably even some remaining Philistines. The fact that many imports from lands such as Greece were found indicated that the Persian city here was quite cosmopolitan in character. Extraordinary is also a large dog cemetery, containing more than 250 dog burials, possibly associated with some sort of religious activity involving canines.

In the Shephelah and Negev, evidence of Persian forts or settlements has appeared at Tell el-Hesi and Lahav, among other sites. Excavations at Tell Jemmeh in particular have uncovered remains of substantial buildings as well as several granaries. The southern parts of the country were consequently also well occupied during this period.

Further inland, Lachish produced a prominent building in the uppermost level of the mound, called the Residency by the excavators. This building, too, was evidently a center for local government administration during this period. At many sites in the hill country, Taanach being one example, Persian occupation was represented by scattered buildings that again were most likely employed for governmental purposes. At the same time, village houses were often found at many sites, such as at Tell es-Sa'idiyeh in the Jordan valley, where a good many mudbrick domestic structures were found. The large building at Tell es-Sa'idiyeh called the "square building" must have been an administrative facility at this same site. Other Persian evidence was found as far south as 'En-Gedi along the Dead Sea, where a settlement dating mainly to this period was found at nearby Tel Goren.

Figure 11.1. Unearthing a Persian dog burial at Ashkelon.

Jordan, however, had a different picture from that west of the Jordan River during the Persian period. Although Persian occupation was present in the Jordan valley and at a limited number of sites, such as Tell Hesban on the plateau, in the highlands south and north of Amman little evidence of a strong Persian administrative presence has appeared. This suggests that the Persians left this region much to itself, probably because they did not foresee any threats to the security of this more remote region. The wealthy Tobiad family mentioned below played an important administrative role in the immediate area of modern Amman, but on the whole the Jordan highlands witnessed the continual development of the local cultures of the Iron Age.

That does not mean, however, that Jordan was completely isolated during this period. On the contrary, a single cuneiform tablet found in the excavations at Tawilan near Petra has opened up a new window into life on the Transjordan plateau during this period. The Tawilan tablet, dated to the time of a Darius (which Darius was not clear), contained a record of a business transaction between the people of Tawilan and the city of Harran in Turkey. This has suggested to archaeologists, therefore, that even though Jordan was not as cosmopolitan as the coastal cities of Palestine, some far-reaching commercial activity did take place from this region during the Persian period.

JERUSALEM AT THE TIME OF THE PERSIAN EMPIRE

According to the Book of Nehemiah, the walls of Jerusalem were reconstructed under Nehemiah's leadership. As the biblical text describes him, Nehemiah led a determined group of exiles back to Jerusalem for the purpose of reestablishing the city's defense system. Since the Book of Nehemiah mentions a date during the reign of Artaxerxes I, it can be assumed that Nehemiah's activity took place sometime between the middle and the end of the fifth century B.C.E. This would place him during the main part of the Persian occupation of ancient Palestine.

The biblical record arouses curiosity whether anything of Nehemiah's activity might have been preserved in the archaeological remains of Jerusalem. Two recent excavations—one British, the other Israeli—have contributed to the discussion of this problem. Both excavations came upon data from the Persian period, but in neither case was the evidence conclusive for the extent of the city built by Nehemiah. Some fragments of what was apparently a city wall were dated to this period, although wider evidence for what the city was like during the Persian period was scanty.

LOCAL POTTERY OF THE PERSIAN PERIOD

The pottery traditions of this period show a unique combination of a good number of imported vessels from the islands and Greece, along with a number of local vessels. Pottery found at sites along the coast indicated that the people here had outside contacts. Since members of the older Phoenician population were still living in some of these coastal settlements, these groups continued their traditional maritime activities. Pottery found at coastal sites consequently often included vessel types similar to those in Cyprus, Rhodes, and Greece, suggesting that products were shipped between the coastal sites and the islands of the Mediterranean and Aegean seas.

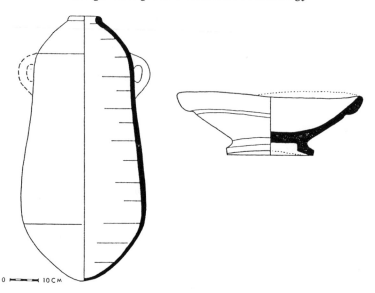

0 ▰▰▰ 10 CM

Figure 11.2. Drawn profiles of a Persian jar and mortarium from Hazor.

In the hill country south and southwest of Jerusalem, where many of the returning exiles had settled, exchange with areas outside the country was more restricted, although occasionally imported vessels appeared here as well. Locally made pottery had less variety, and most vessels of this type served a functional purpose while luxury items were scarce. A predominant vessel was an elongated storage jar that appeared in a number of varieties. These cylindrical vessels were widely dispersed along the eastern Mediterranean during Persian times. In Palestine they have been found at sites along the coast, as well as farther inland at Megiddo, Taanach, Hazor, and Samaria. Their great numbers suggest that they were a common item, probably used for the storage of certain food items.

Another popular vessel was a large bowl sometimes referred to as a *mortarium*, indicating that it may have been used for processing cereal products. These bowls were a local innovation, and no parallels from outside Palestine have been found for them. Since these mortaria have appeared at many sites of the Persian period, they may provide evidence of the importance of cereals in the food lists of people during this period.

SOCIAL CONDITIONS DURING PERSIAN TIMES

Settlement patterns during the Persian period show that the bulk of the land's inhabitants lived away from Jerusalem, even though the rebuilt temple in Jerusalem provided some cohesion to the people of Judah. Many exiles who had returned were involved in working the land. They settled often on the same sites as the previous Iron Age cities or towns, but seem not to have expended great effort at reconstructing these older settlements. Their homes were apparently built to take care of the needs of the moment, while symbols of luxury were for the most part absent during this period. The paucity of archaeological remains having to do with the living situation of the common people of this period suggests that this was by no means a time of abundance for those who had returned. Recent study has shown that the population in Judah during the first half of the Persian period was also quite small. On the other hand, the Jewish population in the hinterland apparently enjoyed greater freedom from the restrictions of the controlling government than those who lived at or near the larger settlements.

The Bible's description of social and economic conditions of the time can be compared to the archaeology of this period. Whereas the books of Ezra and Nehemiah are concerned with religious reformation, both books also contain information on the problems many of the common people experienced in the return of Judean exiles to the land. Ezra 8:1–14 lists the families that returned with Ezra, with the total number of returnees being estimated at about five thousand. Although Ezra enrolled these groups in his program of reconstituting the temple worship and law in Jerusalem, the list suggests that many of those named were laypeople who were concerned first and foremost with the problems of making a living when they returned to their native land.

Precisely that problem is taken up in the Book of Nehemiah (Nehemiah 5). Only a short time after the return of some of the exiles, a devastating famine attacked the area. In addition, taxation by the Persian state was a burden, especially for those who possessed little. Many returning families found themselves in debt to those who had never left the land and ended up pawning

151

property and possessions. Some even offered their sons and daughters as payment for their debts.

These social conditions have received illumination from some important writings found in a cave in the hill country near the Persian settlement at Samaria. The writings were fragmentary scrolls, called the "Wadi edh-Dhaliyeh papyri" after the wadi along which they were found. They were written toward the latter part of the Persian period, that is, during the fourth century B.C.E. They contained a description of how the country was administered by a local official named Sanballat, whose name was the same as that of the earlier foe of Nehemiah (Neh. 4:1–9). The documents contained records of transactions affecting the lives of people in the region of Samaria. A good number of the documents were concerned with the problems of slaves, while others dealt with loans and debts, both major social concerns of the Book of Nehemiah, as has been seen above.

Although Judah had its own independent governmental administration during the Persian period, people in the hilly areas in particular did not seem to have available the resources to undertake larger building projects. Time and energy had to be spent on subsistence. The foremost need, therefore, was not the construction of towns along the old Iron Age lines, but the production of foodstuffs. Excavations have shown that the sites of this period were smaller. Occasionally a wall might be built around the settlement, but nothing like those of earlier cities. As outsiders, the Persians themselves made little effort to settle new parts of the country. They often chose the great old sites of the Bronze and Iron ages on which to establish their settlements, and thus many of the old remains were built over with structures of this period.

THE AGE OF HELLENISM

The Persian dominance in the Near East was destined to pass to a stronger successor. Alexander the Great's military successes in the Near and Far East were some of the swiftest ever to occur in these regions. Beginning with the victory over the Persian forces in the Plain of Issus in November 333 B.C.E., the Greek armies took possession of the entire region from the upper reaches of the Euphrates and Tigris to the Nile in Egypt. The

Near Eastern world now began to learn a new culture and language that would leave their mark into modern times.

It is extraordinary that one person's life could so affect a large region of the world. Not only did Alexander's armies overcome great expanses of Near Eastern territory but, following his death, the cultural influences of Hellenism were assured by the way his kingdom was divided between his military leaders. In this connection Palestine came under the dominance of the Syrian family called the Seleucids, who were adherents of the new culture. Thus, once more Palestine was to find its destiny controlled by external forces.

Although the beliefs and practices of Judaism were strong enough to hold their own over against Greek culture, it seems that the local population often found it difficult to develop its own aspirations during this period. Energy had to be devoted to survival in a situation of occupation. When all the archaeological results of this period are tabulated, it has to be said that we have amazingly little information regarding it. Some of this lack may have come from the fact that Hellenistic remains were usually toward the tops of the mounds and thus could be easily eroded. But that condition can hardly account for so many sites where Hellenistic remains were in a poor state. More likely, local initiatives were often thwarted by bureaucracy or outright suppression, so that Palestine during this period fell back into a period of regression.

ARCHAEOLOGICAL SITES OF THE HELLENISTIC PERIOD

Nonetheless, a number of strategically located sites with substantial settlements were established during this period. One of

The times of Alexander the Great and his successors, the Ptolemies and Seleucids, are indicated in the biblical Book of Daniel. The fourth beast in Daniel 7:7 that broke many kingdoms is a reference to Alexander, just as the ten horns were his successors. The "little horn" in Daniel 7:8 is clearly Antiochus IV Epiphanes, whose destructive policies against the Jews were a major factor in the revolt led by Judas Maccabeus.

Figure 11.3. Hellenistic tower at the entry to Samaria.

these was Samaria in the heart of the hill country of Palestine. During excavations on the north side of the city at Samaria a round tower was exposed. This tower was attached to a fortification wall that surrounded the Hellenistic city, suggesting that Samaria was a center of government administration in the hill country beginning at about 300 B.C.E. Rebuildings and additions to the city occurred during the later phases of the Hellenistic period.

As in the preceding Persian period, the Mediterranean coastal area was a region where Hellenistic settlement was also undertaken. At the harbor site of Dor, a settlement has also been identified by archaeological excavation and survey. As one of the few places along the coast that could be used as a harbor,

Dor was a participant in maritime trade across the Mediterranean. Underwater exploration in the harbor at Dor has brought to light several ship remains, along with a series of anchors representing different periods.

Only a few miles south of Dor was the larger harbor site of Caesarea Maritima, whose heyday was to come during the Roman and Crusader periods but which was also first used during the Hellenistic period. At this time the possibilities of a harbor were first exploited, and a tower called "Straton's town" was built. Other building remains dating to the Hellenistic period have been found in different parts of the site, along with pottery typical of the Hellenistic period.

Although this period was an erratic time for many in the local population, it was also one during which individuals and groups could exploit the circumstances of foreign control. These very conditions gave rise to the serious religious controversies that occurred in Judaism during this period. Those who knew how to adapt themselves to the foreign powers, although looked at suspiciously as compromisers, could attain considerable wealth. Two excavated Hellenistic sites in particular have given impressive evidence of the kind of affluence that could be achieved by people in several regions of the country.

The first is a site in Jordan known by its Arabic name as 'Araq el-Emir. Located in the hills above the Jordan River valley west of Amman, 'Araq el-Emir had a settlement spread out over the hills. In a prominent valley area was a large building, probably a temple. Into the façade of one side of the building was placed a sculptured slab of a cat-like animal, possibly a leopard or lion. This was elegantly carved from red and white dolomite stone with a style suggesting Greek elements. A prestigious Jewish family called the family of Tobiad had long lived in this region, and the wealth of the site of 'Araq el-Emir suggests that the Tobiads did very well during the time of Greek occupation.

A second prominent settlement of the Hellenistic period has been excavated at Tel Anafa located on the edge of the Huleh basin in the northern part of Israel. Excavations at this site have shown that a wealthy city existed here through much of the Hellenistic period. The city was made up of well-constructed buildings often with great amounts of exquisite Hellenistic glassware and pottery in them. What this city was called in antiquity is unknown, but that it was an important location on a main highway trunk to Syria probably accounts for its apparent wealth.

An entire stratum of building activity in Jerusalem was also attributed to the Hellenistic period by the excavators. This included a fortification wall that ringed the city of Jerusalem at this time, and into which was built a large tower at the south end of the city. Within the citadel near the Jaffa Gate, excavation has uncovered part of the Late Hellenistic city wall, into which Herod the Great later inserted the three famous towers of the citadel, still seen today.

POTTERY AND COINS OF THE HELLENISTIC PERIOD

The Hellenistic period is an outstanding one for pottery since a number of unique forms appeared during this period. In many cases these were forms directly imported from the islands or from Greece itself, or they were locally made pieces inspired by Greek types.

One of the most prominent and important vessels was a large storage jar with two thick elongated handles on the sides. The handles of jars of this type were usually stamped with an inscription written in Greek, and thus they have great historical importance. The jars were made in Rhodes and were used to ship wine from that island. Handles of this type have been found by the hundreds at sites in many parts of the country. A great number have come from coastal sites, but many were found in Jerusalem and other inland sites. Perhaps most telling were the large numbers found at Tell er-Rumeith in northern Jordan, pointing to the widespread dissemination of this product.

During the latter part of the Hellenistic period a type of decorated pottery called *terra sigillata* began to appear, continuing into Roman times. This was a very popular ware and was widespread in Europe. In the east it developed its own characteristics that distinguished it from pottery of the same general type made in the west. Along with this pottery was a bowl type decorated with impressed designs of plants or rosettes. Called Megarian bowls, these vessels have been found at sites such as Jericho and Samaria. The origin of this type of bowl was Athens, but local adaptations of it were made in centers such as Antioch in Syria.

It is also important to mention the coinage found during this period, since the number of coins in Palestine dating to the Hellenistic period is enormous. The practice of minting coins was found earlier in Greece, and the earliest coin found in Palestine was a Greek coin found at Shechem and dated to the sixth century B.C.E. Coinage was produced during the Persian period in Palestine, and examples containing the word *Yehud* have been from this period. During the Hellenistic period the rulers of the house of the Hasmoneans had coins minted with their names and images, so that the historical sequence of coins during this period is of great importance.

The use of coinage was also socially and politically important. It suggests an increasing role of the state. The old bartering

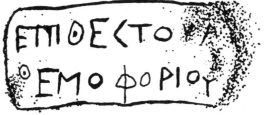

Figure 11.4. Rhodian jar handle from 'Araq el-Emir, reading "(term of) Thestor, (month of) Thesmophorios."

systems were based on individual exchange, and control over the process of exchange was left up to individual relationships. With a uniform system of coinage, such as that found during this period, the regulations of government were clearly more evident. While this had some beneficial effects, it also signified the intrusion of government into everyday life. The times of the Ptolemies and Seleucids in their control of the Near Eastern regions, depicted on numerous coins, were not easy ones for the local populations.

INTERNATIONALISM DURING THE HELLENISTIC PERIOD

During the Hellenistic Age a new pattern began to be set for Palestine. Previously, during the Babylonian and Persian administration of the country, much of the trade activity and political interchange was oriented toward the north and east, and control was often exerted from that direction. With the coming of Hellenism, the dominant influence began to come from the world of the Mediterranean. Now Palestine would turn almost wholly toward the sea, and its relations would be with the west more than the east. Not that it was without such activity formerly; we have seen during earlier periods that the relations with Cyprus and Crete, and certainly the Phoenicians, brought a seaward-looking influence to Palestinian internationalism. Nonetheless, the Hellenistic period opened a new relation with the western regions, and that would continue with the coming of the Romans.

THE JEWISH REVOLT

Of the Seleucid and Ptolemaic kings who followed Alexander, it was Antiochus IV who ended up carrying out a vendetta against the Jewish population. Years of conflict within the Jewish community between the *hasidim* ("faithful ones") and those who compromised with the regime had helped to open the way for Antiochus's persecutions. These oppressions included the desecration of the temple in Jerusalem, the enforced identification of the God of the Jews with Zeus, and the placing of severe restrictions on Jewish worship and practice.

Such policies sparked a resistance movement that eventually brought Antiochus down in defeat. The leaders of the revolt were members of a family living in the small town of Modin, west of Jerusalem in the direction of the Mediterranean Sea. The people were known as the Hasmoneans, and their renowned leader was Judas Maccabeus. The period is also known as the time of the Maccabean revolt, an insurrection carried out under Judas's leadership. Archaeological finds dating from approximately 180 B.C.E. to the latter part of the second century evidence the turbulence of this period. One such site was Beth-zur located in the hills of Judah south of Jerusalem. In the excavations at Beth-zur, a number of structures were uncovered that date to the period of the Maccabees. One was a fortress-like building that may have been used by Judas's men as they prepared themselves for the attack against the Syrian occupants of Jerusalem.

Although the Hasmoneans experienced victory for a short time, and even went so far as to try to reestablish a state modeled on the ancient one of David, their attempts were short-lived. Very soon it became necessary again to live in alignment with the occupying powers. The story of the Jews in Palestine from about 167 to 63 B.C.E. was one of tradeoffs, and it was this tendency to accommodate that provoked the disputes lying behind the Dead Sea Scrolls. The pattern of occupation was to continue into the following period, that of the Romans.

12
The Coming of Rome

Anyone examining the archaeological remains of the Roman Empire cannot but be impressed by the Roman ability in social organization and engineering. To be sure, the Romans were indebted to the Greeks who preceded them, receiving from them influences in their art and architecture as well as in city planning. The development of Roman literature was also shaped in some ways by that of the Greeks. Nonetheless, the Romans gave their peculiar stamp to everything they touched, and their achievements, as can be seen also in Palestine, were substantial.

Palestine was to receive a strong impetus from this direction beginning in the year 63 B.C.E., for it was in that year that the Roman military leader Pompey brought his army to the Middle East. That date thus marked a significant turning point in the history of Palestine. Now the tightly developed system of Roman governance in its various colonies was to influence the course of Palestine's development well into the Christian era.

So extensive are the Roman remains that it is necessary to limit ourselves to the main features, and to note especially the social implications of the archaeological evidence we possess.

THE ROMAN ROAD SYSTEM

We begin with one of the most important engineering feats of the Romans, their system of roads. It would be a mistake to conclude that the Romans were the first to introduce highways

Early Roman	63 B.C.E.–135 C.E.
Middle Roman	135–250 C.E.
Late Roman	250–360 C.E.

160

into Palestine. Archaeological and literary evidence has been able to trace earlier roadways in different parts of the country. As early as the Chalcolithic and Early Bronze ages routes connected different settlements and cities. And by the time of the Late Bronze Age, major highways, such as the one passing from eastern Egypt along the Palestinian coast to Lebanon and Syria, were well established.

Much of the evidence of roads before the Roman period rests on assumption, however, given the scanty remains of these earlier systems. Since the Roman highway engineers often followed the ancient routes, their constructions removed traces of earlier roadways that were commonly made of an earthen base. With the Romans, road technology was given a new impetus. Large numbers of workers were employed in road construction and maintenance. We can also assume that the military was involved in keeping the roads in condition, since the roadways played an important role in transporting the armies and their equipment.

Sea transport was also important to the Romans. We know of their achievements in this area because Roman pottery has been discovered in shipwrecks along the coasts of the eastern Mediterranean. But it was the roadways that would have a particular effect upon the economic and social conditions of the Middle East, and specifically of Palestine. The Roman engineers took pains to construct durable surfaces. Cobblestones or larger pavement stones were commonly used for major roads, while smaller trunk roads sometimes employed a gravel base. Vehicular traffic consisted of horse-drawn wagons, donkeys, and mounted horses. In addition, there was always a great amount of pedestrian traffic.

Sections of Roman road are still traceable in some places west of the Jordan River. A segment of a road connecting the hill country city of Sebaste (modern Sebastya) with Jerusalem was discovered in the plain west of the city. Built above the ruins of ancient Samaria, Sebaste was one of two cities founded by Herod in honor of the Roman emperor Augustus. The other city, Caesarea, lay along the Mediterranean coast. It was also located near the important ancient highway called "the way of the sea" (*Via Maris*), little of which remains today.

The extensive system of Roman highways brought the different parts of the eastern Mediterranean world into contact with each other as never before. Tracing these road systems has opened up many new vistas on Roman occupation of Palestine during the centuries following Pompey's invasion in 63 B.C.E. This was not only the period of the gospels and letters of the New Testament, but included Jewish apocryphal and pseude-pigraphic writings. The Jewish historian Josephus also wrote important accounts at this time.

Jordan also has well-preserved examples of the Roman road system, particularly in some of the isolated and relatively un-disturbed sections of the country. Although not on the main road, which was four miles to the west, the large Roman and Byzantine town of Umm al-Jamal in northern Jordan was linked by means of a secondary road with cities to the northeast and south. Other sections of Roman road are visible south of Amman along what is still today called the King's Highway (*Tarikh al-Malik*), the name for the old Iron Age roadway that in Roman times became incorporated into a system through Transjordan leading to Arabia and Egypt.

Part of a highway can be seen near Tell Hesban at the site of Roman Esbus, a city known from texts to have been along the main Roman route of Transjordan. Farther south near the Wadi Mojib are surviving sections of Roman roadway, and even beyond that preserved sections can be seen in the direction of 'Aila (present-day Aqaba). The best sections, however, have been found south of Kerak and west of modern Ma'an. Here not only remains of the main road but also secondary arteries are visible as they run through the fields of Transjordan. As modern ag-ricultural development spreads, however, it can hardly be ex-pected that remnants of these roads will long survive.

Alongside the ancient Roman roads are often Roman mile-stones. These are cylindrical pillars, sometimes bearing an in-scription and marking distances along these highways. These Roman milestones tell a significant story about the social and political history of this period. They indicate that governmental structures were never far away, and this had implications for

Figure 12.1. Broken Roman milestone on the King's Highway in Jordan.

peasants and villagers living in these regions. Although the quality of highway construction attests a high standard of living during Roman times, at the same time taxes had to be imposed on the local population to support public works of this kind, and thus the advantages were often offset by the costs of maintaining these roads.

TRADE AND EXCHANGE DURING ROMAN TIMES

The road system created new possibilities for commerce and trade. The wide variety of imported articles and vessels in which

163

they were transported is striking. Evidently, Palestine received goodly numbers of imports from Italy and other areas of the Mediterranean. These were shipped by boat but then transported to outlying places across the various highways. Exotic pottery, vessels called *terra sigillata* wares, were sometimes of the type deriving from the western part of the empire, although a variety of eastern sigillata was made locally. The word *sigillum* refers to a potter's mark that is sometimes found on these wares.

The Romans also perfected the glass industry. Although experiments in glass production had been made by earlier peoples, such as the Phoenicians, the technique of glass-blowing in the eastern Mediterranean dates to about the middle of the first century B.C.E. Having mastered this technique, Roman glass-blowers were able to produce a variety of elegant vessels. Among the many types were delicately thin vessels of azure blue or green color. These were coveted as luxury pieces and were widely exported.

Shipwreck archaeology along the Mediterranean coastal areas has brought to light evidence of exported products from Palestine. Large quantities of wine and olive oil were sent to other regions of the Mediterranean, and this also brought income into the country. Underwater archaeology off the coast of sites such as Caesarea has produced many examples of the large storage jars in which items were shipped from Palestine.

ROMAN AQUEDUCTS AND WATER SYSTEMS

Parallel to the Roman system of highways were their aqueducts and related water storage and transport facilities. The conveyance of water from lucrative sources to locations where it was needed was a supreme accomplishment of Roman technology. In societies where government-supported systems of water management are minimal or nonexistent, people must transport their water supplies themselves. This was the case during many of the earlier periods, including that of the Iron Age. It was common during these early periods for a village or town to be located near a spring from which inhabitants could draw water. In the course of time cisterns were also dug, and with the development of water-impervious plaster it became possible to dig cisterns in many previously uninhabited regions of the country.

Under the Roman control of Palestine the government stepped in, as it had in the case of the road system. For it was the availability of water that made the difference in the settlement possibilities and the establishment of new cities along the major highways. Water management thus extended Rome's control over the region.

Roman aqueducts have long been known in Palestine. Several have been investigated by archaeologists, including one spectacular system paralleling the Mediterranean coast north of Caesarea Maritima. This latter city was a Roman government center, serving at one point as the residence of Pontius Pilate. It was also a significant port or harbor city, but it lacked a local water supply, being situated on the *kurkar* sand of the coastal area. Ingeniously the Roman engineers brought water from a spring northeast of Caesarea, channeling it through a major carrying system for almost four miles to the Caesarea site. In many ways

Figure 12.2. Roman aqueduct at Caesarea Maritima.

it was the effectiveness of this water facility that allowed the city of Caesarea to develop.

A second example is a recently investigated aqueduct system in the far south of Jordan. The remote site of Humeima, known as Auara during Roman times, had little to commend it for settlement. The region is desertic and very isolated. Yet the construction of an aqueduct system for conducting water from a major spring in the hills more than fifteen miles distant made possible a thriving settlement at Humeima. The aqueduct was built originally by the Nabataeans, a prosperous Arab people during Roman times, and then maintained all the way through to the Byzantine and Umayyad periods. The main Roman road to 'Aila on the Red Sea (today's Aqaba) also ran through Humeima.

THE ROMAN FORTS

The significance of such Roman towns as Humeima has been debated in recent years. One expedition in Jordan has devoted a series of excavation campaigns and surveys to the problem of explaining the line of Roman settlements stretching along the western edge of the Jordan desert. Most of these settlements served a military purpose, and thus the goal has been to clarify what function the military had at these eastern sites. Examples are found at Lejjun, east of the modern town of Kerak, Dajania, and Humeima. Lejjun has been most extensively excavated, its Roman settlement including large military barracks alongside other buildings.

One theory has held that the Romans placed their forts along the eastern frontier because of threats from desert intruders such as the Saracens. The forts were thus meant to serve as a *limes*, or line of military posts along the eastern border, to keep such peoples under control. Others have argued, however, that the relations between Romans and Saracens did not necessitate such a system of protection. They also have pointed out that the forts are spaced too far apart to have been effective as a "wall" preventing penetration by an unfriendly group. However these forts are to be interpreted, they clearly evidence some form of widespread government control during Roman times.

ROMAN CITIES OF PALESTINE

A major Roman city of Palestine was Caesarea Philippi, located near the Lebanese border. During Roman times this city, visited by Jesus and his disciples, was a center for the worship of the god Pan, from which has come the site's modern name, Banias. A number of cuttings made in the rocky scarp behind the spring at the site were associated with the cult of this god. Farther south along the Mediterranean coast were the harbor cities of Dor and Caesarea Maritima, with their imposing ruins. Located north of Caesarea Maritima, the jetties making possible Dor's harbor facilities have recently been examined. Dor was thus an important emporium for trade with the west.

Caesarea Maritima was one of the great Roman cities of ancient Palestine. Even more so than Dor, Caesarea established harbor facilities that gave it continuous contact with the Mediterranean world. It was from Caesarea that the apostle Paul set out on his final journey to Rome. Large storage areas for imported goods and for government processing and storing goods have been found in the recent excavations. Roman statuary is also abundant at the site, and a Roman theater was situated in such a way that its audience could look beyond the stage to the Mediterranean Sea beyond. Caesarea was a favorite city of Herod the Great; it was also the official residence of the Roman procurator Pontius Pilate.

THE TEMPLE OF HEROD

Among the Roman cities of Palestine, however, none has quite the importance for historical and religious reasons as the city of Jerusalem. Much effort has been spent over the years on archaeological work dealing with the Jerusalem of Jesus' time, and efforts have been made to reconstruct the plan of the city as it was in the first century of the Christian era. Probably the place to begin in discussing Roman or New Testament Jerusalem is the area that is best known from the New Testament, the Herodian temple.

Over the years a number of models of what the temple area of Jesus' time may have looked like have been constructed, based primarily on descriptions in the Bible and other sources as well as on a small amount of archaeological evidence. As a result of extensive excavations made on the temple mount during recent years, we are now able to gain a reasonably good idea of what the temple area was like during New Testament times. An important key has been "Robinson's arch" that protruded from the southern section of the western wall. This feature consisted of a short span of arch projecting from the wall first noted by Edward Robinson during the nineteenth century. Until recently, this arch was thought to have been part of a bridge that crossed the Tyropoean valley west of the temple area. The recent excavations, however, have discovered a matching pier to the west, so that it now seems likely that Robinson's arch, like the newly discovered pier, served as the base for a stairway leading to the temple area on the west side. Worshipers consequently entered the area of the temple from this side, just as they also could have entered by means of a flight of stairs from the south.

The temple itself has to be recreated from textual descriptions, since no evidence of it survives where the Muslim Dome of the Rock stands today. Yet a number of details are provided in New Testament accounts and contemporary descriptions. More important than the actual architectural plan of the Jerusalem temple in Roman times (often referred to as the "Herodian temple" as over against the earlier one built by Solomon and destroyed by the Babylonians) is the function of the temple in the Jerusalem of the first century C.E.

In the ancient Near East, temples were built as houses for the god or goddess, not as meeting places for a religious community. The temple had broad social, political, and economic meaning. Temples served as the focus of a city, and the main components of a society were integrated around this religious center. The temple provided a firm basis for the society and its governance, since the deity who resided there, or who made intermittent appearances, was the force undergirding all aspects of the society's welfare. The priests who oversaw the ceremonies of the temple also had an important function in maintaining the stability of the society that the temple served.

The temple of Jesus' time was constructed by Herod the Great and dedicated in the year 30 B.C.E. Like other Near Eastern temples, Herod's temple had religious and political meaning. The

Figure 12.3. The landmark Dome of the Rock on the temple site of ancient Jerusalem.

Jewish population that had experienced turmoil since the days of Babylonian destruction could be brought more securely under control through the integrating power of this central feature of Jewish worship. The temple in Jesus' time was thus a building and a sacred area around which much of Jewish life in all of its aspects centered.

JERUSALEM IN JESUS' TIME

How often Jesus was in Jerusalem is not clear from the Gospels, which have differing information on this subject. All four Gospels agree that the final week of his life was spent in Jerusalem, and it seems that it was during this week that he made his threatening statements against the temple. Jesus' negative words about the temple, however, were colored by later events closer to the actual destruction of the temple some forty years later. For it was in 70 C.E. that the Roman armies under Titus finally invaded the city of Jerusalem, took the treasures of the temple as booty, and burned and destroyed it. The event was then celebrated with the construction of the Titus Arch in the forum in Rome. After 70 C.E. the temple mountain stood empty until the late seventh century saw the erection of the famous Islamic mosque known as the Dome of the Rock (*kubbat es-sakra*).

Other aspects of the Roman period in Jerusalem have become clear through recent archaeology. In addition to work undertaken in the temple mount area, excavation has clarified water reservoirs built below the city during Herod's time. Since Jerusalem did not always have an adequate water supply, particularly as the population grew, Herod's engineers were able to bring water from what is today known as "Solomon's pools," located approximately halfway between Bethlehem and Hebron, all the way to Jerusalem. Although the Gihon spring continued to be used as a source of water during the Roman period, it could not produce enough water for the growing population of Jerusalem. The Herodian system of water storage met this need, and thus was a considerable achievement.

The Roman ruins below the modern city of Jerusalem give us some idea of the difficulties of archaeological work in this city. In reality we know more about the second century C.E. Roman city than that of the time of Jesus. It seems that the gate at the north end of the city, brought to light through excavation below the present Damascus Gate, was a first-century feature of the city. The recently restored *cardo maximus* presents us with the city of the second century, but it is possible to make some assumptions about what the city was like during the days of Jesus by extrapolating from the ruins and plan of the somewhat later city.

THE SITE OF THE CHURCH OF
THE HOLY SEPULCHRE IN JERUSALEM

For Christians, the problem of the burial place of Jesus and the location of the ancient hill on which he died have been matters with which New Testament archaeology has been concerned. In

Figure 12.4. Roman Gate below the Damascus Gate in Jerusalem.

recent years a great deal of work has been done in exposing earlier sections of the Church of the Holy Sepulchre, covered over by later construction. Parts of this church date back to the first half of the fourth century c.e. when Palestine became part of the Byzantine empire. At that time, Constantine's mother Helena undertook the consecration of sites thought to be the locations of important occurrences during Jesus' ministry. Archaeology devoted to the Church of the Holy Sepulchre has restored several parts of the church that originated at the time of Helena.

Helena's intention in Jerusalem was to build a church over the place of Jesus' burial. Naturally the question arises whether the site of this church has validity as being the site of this final event in the ministry of Jesus. Although many cautions are attached by archaeologists to their conclusions, a certain amount of consensus exists that the church was indeed in that part of Jerusalem that would have been a logical place for the execution of criminals. The site of the Church of the Holy Sepulchre was, in other words, outside the walls of the city at that time, a necessary condition for the events that occurred there. In addition, tombs dating to the first century have been found in the area around the church, one such tomb being found off to the side of the spot that is venerated by pilgrims today as the place of Jesus' tomb.

Obviously this evidence does not prove that any one of these tombs was the tomb of Jesus. Such specificity is impossible to establish. Nor can archaeological evidence offer anything about the validity of the belief in Jesus' resurrection, a matter that lies beyond the efforts of archaeologists. What is indicated is that there was a tradition about the site of the Church of the Holy Sepulchre that went back to at least the fourth century of the Christian era. And most archaeologists would agree that the tradition of Jesus' burial at this site would have been older than that, since it was well established by the time Helena made the decision to build a church on the site.

If the Church of the Holy Sepulchre may have been the site of the final events of Jesus' life, then other parts of the account of the last week of his ministry might also be filled in, again not with any kind of absolute certainty. The archaeology of New Testament Jerusalem has dealt with the problem of where Jesus was brought before the Roman tribunal, the so-called Praetorium. Archaeologists differ on the location of this building, some holding to the Fortress Antonia on the east side of the city, others to the Citadel on the west. The route taken from this building, wherever it was located, to Calvary is also part of the discussion of these events. These are matters that have been much obscured through the centuries by Christian tradition and piety, and yet they belong to an important part of early Christian archaeology in Palestine.

THE DECAPOLIS CITIES

During Roman times there existed a group of cities that played an important role in the history of Roman occupation, and that were also sometimes significant in the life of Jesus and the early Christian church. These are the cities known as the Decapolis (the "ten cities"). Several are mentioned in the New Testament, and today a number of them have been investigated by archaeologists. With one exception, Scythopolis, these cities were located east of the river Jordan. They were important in the economic and political arrangements of the Romans in Palestine.

In the southern part of the Decapolis region was Philadelphia, identified with modern Amman. Of the Decapolis cities that have been explored, one of the most accessible is Gerasa, north of Amman. Known today as Jerash, it is a popular stopping place for visitors to Jordan, since it is one of the best preserved Roman cities in the Middle East. Much that is seen at Jerash today, however, was not there in the days of Jesus. The ruins seen today are largely those of the city created for the royal visit of the emperor Hadrian (117–138 C.E.). It was also at Hadrian's time that the city of Jerusalem was rebuilt as Aelia Capitolina, in connection with this emperor's visit. Nevertheless, some first-century Roman evidence is present at Jerash, such as the temple of Zeus that was the original sanctuary of this important site.

Another city of the Decapolis recently under excavation is ancient Gadara. Known today as Um Qeis, this was a site of great wealth during Roman times. Again, much that is seen at Um Qeis, such as its two theaters and monumental gate, is from the second and third centuries. But evidence also exists of the first-century city that stood here at the time of Jesus. Nearby on the north side of Um Qeis is the extraordinary Roman bath at Hammat Gader, the baths of the city of Gadara. This is just one example of the many Roman establishments around hot springs. It was a tradition among Romans to locate the natural hot springs and build spas in connection with them. Herod the Great founded the same type of baths at Callirhoe on the eastern shore of the Dead Sea.

The system of Decapolis cities, then, is another testimony to Roman administration during the time they controlled Palestine. The Decapolis cities offered an effective protective shield along

Figure 12.5 Roman thermal baths at Hammat Gader.

the eastern border of Roman Palestine, on the edge of the great desert that runs to the east. In a similar way as the Roman camps stretched along the eastern border in the south of Jordan, these cities effectively managed Roman control and Roman administration. They also provided a convenient and valuable linkage for commerce and travel, together with the road system connecting these cities.

THE NABATAEAN CITY OF PETRA IN JORDAN

Attention should be drawn to one last city located in Jordan, the city of Petra. Without question the ruins of Petra are one of the archaeological treasures of the Middle East, and it is not surprising that Petra has become an essential stopping place for those visiting Jordan. Nothing quite like it can be found anywhere else. The city of Petra was carved into the colorful Nubian sandstone of the mountainous rock that overlooks the Araba to the west. The notion of making such a city out of sandstone was conceived by the people who lived in this region, the Nabataeans, an Arab people involved in trade between Syria and Mesopotamia and between Arabia and Egypt.

The Nabataeans at first used Petra as a burial area, cutting tombs into its sandstone. But soon such activity suggested carving elaborately shaped façades of other types, along with freestanding structures such as temples, high places, and administration centers. Nabataean activity continued into the Roman period, at which time Petra came eventually under Roman control. During Roman times a city was established in the usual way, with a *cardo maximus* providing the main axis of the city. A theater in the Roman tradition was also constructed. Petra is a legacy of engineering brilliance, first by the Nabataeans who conceived the idea of such a city, and later the Romans, who in their manner organized this city the way it is viewed today.

13
Jews and Christians during Roman and Byzantine Times

The developments in Christianity that followed Jesus' ministry brought about another new era in the history of Palestine. While the Christian movement was at first within the framework of Judaism, under the influence of leaders such as Paul the church community began to spread broadly among non-Jews. Alongside its mission activity, Christianity proceeded to define itself as a unique institution rather than as a sectarian group within the Jewish community. Meanwhile, Judaism continued in one of the most formative periods of its history.

As far as the archaeology of the first several centuries of Christian-Jewish relations in Palestine is concerned, we are only recently in possession of important information. This period, long neglected by archaeologists more interested in earlier times, is now coming into its own with the promise of much new material clarifying the relation between the two communities during the early centuries of Christianity. Much of this information casts new light on the social composition of both communities, on their settlement patterns and locations, as well as on their interrelations. We are indeed at the edge of a new era in the understanding of early Christianity and its relation to the Jewish community from which it emerged.

Early Roman	63 B.C.E.–135 C.E.
Middle Roman	135–250 C.E.
Late Roman	250–360 C.E.
Early Byzantine	360–491 C.E.
Late Byzantine	491–640 C.E.

THE DEAD SEA SCROLLS AND EARLY CHRISTIANITY

The discovery of the scrolls in the caves at Qumran near the Dead Sea has brought about a significant rethinking of the relation of Christianity to Jewish sectarianism. Archaeological discoveries in the caves and at the site of the settlement have helped to show how Jesus and his followers, so closely related to the Jewish eschatologist John the Baptist, became embroiled in the debates within the Jewish community itself during the last centuries B.C.E.

It is still a commonly accepted view that the Jewish community that produced the scrolls was a part of the sect known as the Essenes, although a minority of scholars disputes this. A dissident group, the Essenes rose up in opposition to the main Jewish leadership in Jerusalem. Qumran doctrine held that the Jerusalem leaders had sold out to the political powers of the time. One of their documents, called the "War between the Sons of Light and the Sons of Darkness," depicted a showdown between righteousness and evil before the arrival of the age of the Messiah.

Although it is not yet clear just how the early communities around Jesus and that at Qumran might have been related, certain parallels between the two seem apparent. Comparisons have been made between the ritual washings of the Qumran

Figure 13.1. Fragment of the Book of Daniel from one of the Dead Sea Caves.

covenantors and descriptions in the New Testament of the baptism of John the Baptist. Some scholars have also pointed to the messianic communal meal shared by the Qumran community and its similarities to the supper instituted by Jesus. Also of note have been the commentaries of the Qumran sect on sections of the Hebrew Bible. These commentaries followed procedures similar to the way the New Testament interpreted the older scriptures. An outstanding example of this kind of *pesher* interpretation was an intact scroll containing a commentary on the Book of Habakkuk.

In comparison to Qumran, however, there was something distinctive about Jesus and the community that grew around him. For one thing, the movement at Qumran died out, while that having to do with Jesus not only survived the disappointments of his crucifixion, but spread and expanded. The early Christian community soon came to exist far beyond the confines of Palestine itself.

At the same time that Christianity was establishing itself as a new faith, the Jewish community was also deepening its self-understanding. External pressures such as the invasion of Jerusalem by Titus catalyzed each of these two faiths to a greater concern with their identity, and this also affected their relations with each other. Since the earliest Christians had moved out of traditional Judaism to confess the new faith, their conversion often resulted in debates and conflicts between the Jewish and early Christian communities.

The archaeology of the first centuries of the Christian era thus takes on a special significance when studied in regard to the development of these two communities. Data brought to light by recent expeditions concentrating on the early period of the Christian era suggest new perspectives on the relation between the Jewish and Christian communities during these first centuries of the modern era.

EARLY CHRISTIANITY DURING THE ROMAN PERIOD

Though growing, the Christian church of the first centuries was neither large enough nor wealthy enough to have left significant structures behind. In reality, the earliest Christian communities met in homes often located in the neighborhoods of local synagogues. In addition, the times were as difficult for Christians as they were for the Jewish community. The Roman authorities found the quarrels between the two groups not only disturbing but also threatening to the order imposed upon the area. These tensions also had the result that it was difficult for either community to pursue the construction of buildings on a broad scale.

The result is that we find little evidence of early Christian architecture in Palestine. The earliest Christian building for which we may have evidence is at Capernaum near the Sea of Galilee. This old town was important for the early Christians, since Jesus himself and several of his followers, such as Peter, had been active here. A church in the form of an octagon was built at Capernaum sometime during the second or third century C.E. This is perhaps the earliest Christian church prior to the age of Constantine.

Many other locations important for their association with Jesus were also venerated, although much of the pilgrimage tradition was a development of the Byzantine age. Nonetheless, it seems that the sites that early Christians identified with the crucifixion and Jesus' tomb became important very early, although again without any significant structures having been built during this early period. Bethlehem also may have been revered by early Christians, since evidence dating before the Byzantine period was found in a grotto below the fourth-century Church of the Nativity.

CHRISTIANITY DURING THE BYZANTINE PERIOD

The main information we have on the building of early churches in Palestine dates, however, to the Byzantine period. The earliest examples are the well-known Church of the Nativity in Bethlehem and the Church of the Holy Sepulchre in Jerusalem. Later, as the Christian population of Palestine grew during the fifth and sixth centuries C.E., many churches were built in the Negev, on the Jordan plateau, in the Jordan valley, and several places along the shore of the Dead Sea.

One well-preserved Byzantine site in the Negev was Shivta, a town known during Byzantine times as Subeita. The overall plan of Shivta's Byzantine settlement can still be seen in the well-preserved ruins of the site today. Excavations here have uncovered a complex of domestic, public, and commercial buildings, making it possible to visualize how the people who lived in Subeita in the fifth century organized their lives and daily needs.

The original walls of several churches tower over the ruins of Shivta today. These churches were constructed in the basilica style typical of Eastern churches at the time. At the eastern end of the sanctuary was a central apse, with an additional smaller apse often found on each side of the central one. The main apse constituted the presbytery, for it was here that the presbyters gathered around the altar for the eucharistic celebration. Stretching out to the west was the nave where the members of the congregation gathered. The nave was usually divided by at least two rows of columns forming colonnades on the sides of the nave. Between the nave and presbytery was a screen wall usually made of fine marble separating the nave from the altar. This

Figure 13.2. The Byzantine North Church at Shivta.

screen had the effect of hiding the holiest place of the sanctuary from the eyes of the worshipers. During the worship the celebrants passed through doors in this screen wall, which bears the technical term *iconostasis*.

Churches such as the North and South Churches at Shivta also had baptismal fonts in or near the narthex at the rear of the church. Here the baptismal candidates were received into the church on the night before Easter. Since the fonts had steps leading into them, the practice of baptism in this period was most likely by partial or complete immersion. The baptismal font of the South Church at Shivta was in the form of a cross. The churches at Shivta are some of the best examples we possess of early Christian church architecture in the Byzantine period. Not far away, also in the Negev, was a well-preserved church at Avdat.

Jerusalem was the location of a number of large churches during Byzantine times. The Church of the Holy Sepulchre has already been mentioned. One of the largest churches known in Palestine from this period was also the so-called Nea (New) Church of St. Mary, recently excavated on the southeastern side of the old city of Jerusalem. This church is probably the one indicated on the mosaic map found in a Byzantine church at Madaba in Jordan. Based on inscriptional evidence found in the Nea Church itself, the time of its construction was the sixth century C.E.

The work of a number of large archaeological projects devoted to the study of the Byzantine period in Jordan has demonstrated that many parts of Jordan also witnessed the establishment of Christian towns and villages together with their churches. Churches have been found even in an area as remote as the site of Khirbet es-Samra on the edge of the Jordan desert northeast of Amman. The Byzantine remains at Khirbet es-Samra show that this town had at least three churches. Excavations also showed that the town reached its heyday during the sixth and seventh centuries C.E., declining in the eighth century.

The eastern Jordan valley, too, contained important examples of churches. One of these was at Pella, east of the Jordan River, one of the Decapolis cities. The church at Pella was significant because it was the seat of a bishop. Among other cities of the

Decapolis where churches have been found, Jerash (Gerasa of the New Testament) stands out for its several churches. Others have been excavated at Scythopolis and Abila.

A recently excavated Byzantine church in Jordan also relates to information found on the Madaba Map (see below). It has long been recognized that the map depicts a church near the southeastern shore of the Dead Sea, bearing the name of the holy Lot, or "Saint Lot." Excavations near the southeast Dead Sea have discovered remains of a monastery and church that most probably are those of this church. The discovery of two inscriptions containing the name Lot, and the fact that the site is in the right place to be correlated with the Madaba Map, make this most likely. The correlation between the archaeological information and that on the map is a noteworthy discovery.

MOSAICS IN THE CHURCHES IN JORDAN

The large number of Byzantine churches east of the Jordan River thus suggests that a sizable Christian population was found here between the third and seventh centuries, until the coming of Islam when conversions to the latter faith resulted in decreases in the Christian population. Several churches have been found on Mount Nebo near the northeast end of the Dead Sea. These churches, like others in the Madaba region and elsewhere in the country, usually had lavishly decorated mosaic floors. Study of these mosaics has supplied a vast amount of fresh information regarding the history of the early Christian church during the Byzantine period.

Two mosaics in particular contain important information on the Christian church of this period. The first was the design found in the mosaic floor of the Byzantine church at Madaba, mentioned previously. This famous mosaic, commonly referred to as the Madaba Map, was created when a new church was built in this town during the sixth century C.E. The map on the church floor contains rich geographic information regarding Palestine during this period, including towns named in the Bible and their locations.

Recently, mosaic floors were uncovered in two Byzantine churches excavated at Um er-Rasas along the eastern desert in Jordan. This site was apparently ancient Mephaath mentioned in the Bible (Josh. 13:18). The mosaic in one of the churches depicts the main cities and towns where churches were located. The names of several bishops in the region around Madaba are also given. Dated to shortly after 750 C.E., the Um er-Rasas mosaic provides invaluable information about Christians and their churches during the first centuries of Islam.

BYZANTINE SOCIAL ORGANIZATION

Byzantine Christianity played a significant role in the political and social realities of the period. The church lived by a vision that saw the world as one, governed by an emperor who, while administering human affairs, was also the representative of the royal figure of Christ on earth. This unified conception of the spiritual and temporal world left its mark on the character of Byzantine settlements, whose ruins are studied by archaeologists.

Archaeological excavations and surveys have shown that many parts of Palestine that previously were unused were settled

Figure 13.3. Mosaic at Um er-Rasas, depicting major cities of Palestine with their churches.

Remains of the Byzantine period are found in abundance in modern Jordan and Israel. This was a time during which a high standard of living was found in towns and villages. Byzantine agricultural technology profited from previous experiments in water management by the Romans and Nabataeans, and many parts of the country were turned into habitable regions. Written accounts from this period can be found in early Christian writers such as Eusebius of Caesarea and Cyril of Jerusalem. This was also the period during which the Mishnah and Talmud shaped rabbinic Judaism.

during the Byzantine period. Byzantine technology developed new water-collection systems that were successfully implemented in the desert regions of the Negev and the Dead Sea. People of this period had the benefit of earlier experimentations in water management by the Romans and Nabataeans, the latter in particular having mastered the scarce resources of the desert region. But the Byzantine populations brought a new impetus to desert occupation. They built aqueducts to transport water to desired locations. They perfected cistern and small dam construction. They practiced terracing of the hillsides in order to increase the amount of land that could be planted.

The Byzantine Christian population of Palestine consequently shared in the high standard of living of the empire. Excavation of Byzantine settlements in Palestine shows that this was a flourishing period. The Byzantine populace took over Roman techniques of social organization, adapting these to their own needs and goals. It is not an exaggeration to say that the Byzantine period in Palestine was one of the largest ever (demographically speaking) in many parts of the country.

Despite the fact that Palestine was far from Constantinople, it was tied to the capital through ecclesiastical organization. The bishops and priests supplied the main points of reference, while bishops were at times personally able to represent their regions. The homogeneity of the period was evident in the system of similar settlement patterns, the use of similar techniques in agricultural production, the employment of traditional motifs in church architecture, and the establishment of common forms of local governance within the church. The Byzantine period was a unique one from the standpoint of its social organization.

THE ARCHAEOLOGY OF JUDAISM DURING THE ROMAN AND BYZANTINE PERIODS

The Jewish community also underwent changes during the centuries of early Christianity. Under Roman harassment and persecution Jews also found their membership declining. But this in no sense led to an evacuation of the land by Jews. Excavations of the remarkable Jewish catacomb tombs at Beth Shearim in Galilee have provided evidence of the size and vitality of the Jewish population in Galilee in the third and fourth centuries C.E. The fine Jewish artwork in these tombs is also a sign that Jewish settlement was far from being tentative, and that it was deeply established in this region of the country.

Much like the early Christian community, however, only small amounts of evidence of Jewish architecture dating to the first and second centuries C.E. have survived. This could be simply accidental, but more likely it suggests that the disfavor of the Romans produced an environment not conducive to building activities, as it did in the case of the Christians.

One notable exception was a structure discovered at Masada, which was most likely a synagogue. Built originally during the time of Herod at the end of the first century B.C.E., this building continued to be used well into the first century C.E. The building consisted of a rectangular room with benches lining its walls. Several fragmentary scrolls were found buried in its floor, indicating that the room had also served as a *geniza,* or a storage place for scrolls no longer in use in the synagogue. That the building was oriented toward Jerusalem was also important, since such an orientation followed a rabbinical dictum that synagogues should be aligned with the holy city. The Masada synagogue is important because it is one of the two or three synagogues so far to date to the first century C.E. Other synagogues from the second and third centuries have been uncovered, while the well-preserved one at Capernaum has provoked debate over whether it is to be dated to the third or second century C.E., or, as the excavators have held, to the late fourth or fifth century.

Well over a hundred synagogues have been excavated to date in Israel and the West Bank. Areas where synagogues have been found include Galilee, the Jordan valley, and the west side of the Dead Sea. A large number have also now been traced in the Golan Heights. One synagogue containing a mosaic floor with inscription was discovered near Jericho, while at 'En-Gedi along the western shore of the Dead Sea a further example with mosaic was found. Notably at 'En-Gedi the niche that contained the Ark was found on the north wall facing Jerusalem, just as at Khirbet Shema in the Galilee the niche was found in the south wall facing the holy city. Although not many synagogues have appeared in Jordan, one was found at the large site of Jerash. That this structure was built over by a later church may suggest that the smaller Jewish population of Jordan resettled west of the Jordan River.

Like many of the Byzantine churches, the synagogues of the period often contained mosaics, and these have provided a valuable window into Jewish worship and thought during the early centuries of the Christian era. The Torah instructed that no images were to be made of anything in, above, or below the earth (Deut. 5:8). Since the God of Israel was not among the creatures, the Torah specified the limits of artistic representation. Thus early Jewish art shunned the use of nature themes that might imply that the divinity could be encompassed within the creaturely world.

At the same time, Jewish worship, as known from the Book of Psalms, was often focused on the theme of God as creator of all that exists. Thus, at the same time that there was a prescription against imagery, there existed an openness to the idea of the divine creator who also cares for the creatures of the earth. This notion of "the beneficent creator" was one that stimulated the artists of the synagogue mosaics. The mosaic floors often had colorful depictions of the animal and tree kingdoms, and sometimes even of human forms. Of particular interest was the use in several synagogue mosaics of the signs of the zodiac. These depicted animal figures representing the principal planets affecting human life on the earth during the months of the year. In the synagogue at Beth Alpha in the north of modern Israel the center of the mosaic floor contained the motifs of nature while on the borders were signs of the zodiac. Near the Sea of Galilee at the site of Hammat Gader, a mosaic floor in a synagogue also contained a circle representing the different figures of the zodiac. This use of the zodiac in some of the synagogues shows the influence of Greek mythology during the Roman and Byzantine periods.

At the same time, the fact that motifs in the mosaic art of the synagogues sometimes resembled those found in Christian churches has suggested that Judaism was also influenced by Christian art just as the latter also received influences from the creative developments within synagogue art. These facts indicate an important facet of the interchange between the two communities during the Byzantine period.

THE GALILEE SYNAGOGUES

The region of Galilee was an area with a large Jewish population during the fourth to the sixth centuries C.E. The city of Tiberias along the Sea of Galilee had attracted some of the great sages of Judaism, and was to continue to be a prominent Jewish city well into the Middle Ages. North of the Sea of Galilee in the highlands near Safed were other Jewish towns, several of them populous. A number of them contained outstanding examples of synagogue construction during this period. A major archaeological expedition has concentrated on the study of several of these Galilee synagogues, with examples having been excavated at Meron, Gush Halav (Giscala), Nabratein, and Khirbet Shema.

In general, the Galilee synagogues were similarly constructed in the basilica style, an oblong building tradition originating in Roman times. An exception was the broadhouse building uncovered and restored at Khirbet Shema. Always important for the study of synagogue architecture, as with that of churches, has been the question of the central focus. In the case of synagogues this would have been the Torah scroll, which was deposited in a shrine or ark at a prominent place along one of the walls of the synagogue. Near the ark would have stood the *bema*, or raised platform, from which the Torah was read and public prayers were led. The results of the excavations at the Galilee synagogues have brought new information to light regarding these two major elements in Jewish worship.

Figure 13.4. The synagogue at Khirbet Shema.

An unusual find among the synagogue remains at Nabratein was a unique piece of fractured limestone. The carved figures it contained indicated that it was part of a holy ark that once had held the Torah scroll or scrolls. The piece had apparently broken off from the upper part of the ark. Since it was the first example of such a central item in synagogue worship ever to be found, its importance has been considerable. The art depicted a carved gabled roof, above which were crouching lions on each side, while below were rosettes and a large shell design. It was evident that a chain had originally been inserted through a small opening toward the top, and that this had held the symbolic, everburning light. The study of this interesting piece advances considerably the understanding of early Jewish worship during the Roman and Byzantine periods.

THE ARCHAEOLOGY OF JEWISH-CHRISTIAN RELATIONS

We may ask then, finally, whether archaeology is able to offer any help in understanding interrelations between Jews and Christians during these early centuries. It has already been suggested that the answer is affirmative. The archaeology of the Roman and Byzantine periods has produced a body of new evidence that needs to be integrated into any social study of the two communities. Much of that evidence bears on the contacts that Jews and Christians had with one another in some of the communities of Palestine. If taken seriously, the new information helps correct certain misconceptions that have characterized Jewish-Christian relations following the development of early Christianity.

Of course, differences of interpretation between the two communities were certainly present. And they were sometimes bitter, as the much-discussed anti-Jewish statements of the New Testament show. Part of the explanation for such derogatory expressions, however, involved the fact that both sides were living under Roman oppression. Each party, therefore, was inclined to blame the other for the difficult conditions that were often present. This is not to deny the fact of documented persecution of Jews by Christians, especially later during Byzantine times.

When Justin Martyr, a Christian, attempted to debase Judaism in his *Dialogue with Trypho the Jew,* written sometime around 130 c.e., he certainly had a political purpose in mind in addressing his negative remarks to the emperor. The results of archaeological research suggest, however, that a good deal of the hostility was paper warfare of this type. That is, it represented the viewpoints of individuals or subgroups within each community, but did not always reflect the day-to-day contacts between Christians and Jews. If the settlement-pattern evidence is brought into the discussion, we find that Christians did indeed settle in great numbers east of the Jordan River, while the small number of synagogues east of the river indicates that the Jewish population was small. It can be concluded from this that in some cases the two communities were distanced from each other through their choices of different regions.

But that is only part of the picture. Many Christians also were settled west of the river—in the Negev, the hill country, the

Galilee, and around Jerusalem. In cities such as Beth-shean, known as Scythopolis during the Roman and Byzantine periods, Jews and Christians lived side by side. Excavation at Beth-shean has uncovered several synagogues as well as a monastery, showing considerable population on the part of both groups. Jerusalem was certainly a city that contained many synagogues and churches well into the Byzantine period.

The example of Capernaum has already been pointed to. The proximity of the Christian church and synagogue to one another in this town suggests at the very least that people in Capernaum were able to come to grips with pluralism in their local community. There seems little reason to believe that members of the two communities here did not get along with each other. We might assume that they shopped and conversed together in what archaeology has shown to be their common locale.

This area of archaeological research, therefore, has a special relevance to our modern situation, and we may expect a great deal more discussion of it in the future. Jews and Christians alike have been in Palestine since the earliest centuries. From the very first, their relations to each other have been a challenge, but it is useful to know that they often succeeded in their relationships to one another.

14
Muslims, Christians, and Jews during the Islamic Period

Palestinian archaeologists call the latest period with which they are concerned the "Islamic period." This period began over a thousand years ago, when new states and empires were founded on the basis of the religion of Islam. The period may in one way be said to have ended with the breakup of the Ottoman Empire following World War I, but in another sense it continues into the modern history of the Middle East, with its various states still based to one degree or another on Islamic principles.

The archaeology of the Islamic period unfortunately has sometimes not received the attention it deserves. The cultural remains of this period are commonly the uppermost on a site, and consequently they have sometimes been carelessly dealt with as researchers have excavated down to the earlier materials in which they might have been interested. Fortunately, a good number of Jordanian, Israeli, and foreign archaeologists have recently devoted much effort to this later period. Not only have studies been made of the larger population centers, but increasingly an interest in Arabic village life and culture has emerged.

The religious traditions of Islam were a binding factor in family and community life, affecting social organization and even the layouts of towns and villages. Hence it is possible today to combine archaeological investigation of this period with study of modern villages, whose lifeways are often not greatly different from those of earlier centuries of Islam. Thus, a concern with the archaeology of the Islamic period also has the benefit of deepening our understanding of one of the largest cultural and religious groups existing today.

The Islamic period was the period during which the Crusades took place; therefore, the archaeological remains of Crusader

191

times will figure into the discussion of this chapter. One of our purposes in this chapter will be to look at how archaeology brings new information to bear on the relations among the Muslims, Jews, and Christians of Palestine during the Islamic period.

CHRONOLOGY OF THE ISLAMIC PERIOD

It will help to begin by noting the several dynasties by which the archaeology of this period is discussed by archaeologists and historians. The first such dynasty is that of the Umayyad caliphs, under whom the far-reaching conquests of the early Islamic empire, including Palestine, took place. The Umayyads (sometimes spelled "Omayyads") ruled between 661 and 750 C.E. They established their capital at Damascus, where remnants of buildings dating to this dynasty are still to be found, the most magnificent being the famous Umayyad mosque that captures the interest of visitors to this city today. Many remains of Umayyad activity are scattered throughout modern Israel and Jordan.

With the decline of the Umayyad Dynasty, the center of power shifted to Iraq and the city of Baghdad, where the dynasty of the Abbasids dominated from approximately 750 to 1258 C.E. The Abbasids lost their control of Egypt, however, when the North African Fatimid Dynasty took that country in 969, which also affected Palestine. The Abbasid Dynasty was the time of the Crusades as well, since for almost two centuries, between 1099 and 1291 C.E., Palestine was subjected to five crusades carried on by Christian armies from Europe.

Major changes came swiftly toward the end of the Abbasid Dynasty. In 1169 the military leader Saladin became sultan of Egypt, following his defeat of the Fatimids and the withdrawal

Umayyad Dynasty	661–750 C.E.
Abbasid Dynasty	750–1258 C.E.
Fatimid Dynasty	969–1169 C.E.
Crusader Period	1099–1291 C.E.
Ayyubid Dynasty	1169–1252 C.E.
Mamluk Dynasty	1252–1517 C.E.
Ottoman Empire	1517–1918 C.E.

of the Crusader armies from that country. Saladin's family were descendants of the Kurds in northern Iraq, and had taken the name of one of their famous members, Ayyub. For a brief time, from 1169 to 1252, therefore, Egypt and Palestine were ruled by the Ayyubid successors of Saladin. Then in 1252, the Mamluk Dynasty, under Baybars, assumed control of Egypt from the Ayyubids, governing it along with Palestine until 1517.

Finally, the fourth and last transformation saw the establishment of the four-hundred-year Ottoman Empire. With the end of the Mamluk Dynasty in 1517, the Ottoman Turks founded their extensive empire of which Palestine was a small part. Ottoman control of Palestine continued until the end of World War I, at which time Turkey relinquished its command of the region to the Allied nations. Because the Ottoman Empire was a recent political reality, its archaeological remains have significance for understanding our own period.

POTTERY OF THE ISLAMIC PERIOD

Before looking at the archaeological picture during the different dynasties, it is important to say a few words about the study of pottery and glass of the Islamic period. In contrast to the pottery of most earlier periods, that of the Islamic period has only recently been given intensive study by archaeologists. Elegant wares such as molded pottery of Abbasid times have long been known, but what has been lacking is a pottery typology through the entire Islamic period, based on sites that have been stratigraphically excavated. The absence of such data has hampered study of the Islamic period since, as we saw earlier, pottery styles and decoration are fundamental dating mechanisms for archaeologists. Glassware is more difficult to distinguish, but developments in the study of this art have also recently begun.

A popular feature of Umayyad pottery was a range of painted designs. One found often consisted of red-painted vessels over which were painted simple white designs. Somewhat later, under the Abbassids, a variety of brown-, green-, and yellow-glazed vessels were produced, and a common gray ware also became popular. While the Ayyubid-Mamluk potters continued to make glazed wares, they also introduced new styles of geometric painted decoration. A variety of blue-to-green glasswares was

Figure 14.1. An Umayyad jar from Pella.

also produced during Mamluk times, continuing the glaze tradition of earlier times. During the Ottoman period, a good deal of local village pottery was made, a sign of the social and political realities in Palestine as it became something of a backwater. Heavy vessels called sugar pots were also produced, and have been found at sites where that industry continued into Ottoman times.

THE ISLAMIC CONQUEST AND THE UMAYYAD DYNASTY

The Islamic period began with the new revelation received by the prophet Muhammad, but it was not until after the prophet's death that Islam reached Palestine. Muhammad himself was never able to set foot in Palestine, although there were traditions about a mystical nighttime visit he had made to Jerusalem (Surah 17:1). According to Muslim tradition he also ascended to heaven from the spot where the al-Aqsa mosque in Jerusalem now stands.

As the Islamic armies moved out of Arabia to the north, they were to face some critical encounters with the Byzantine forces. Initially the Arab armies were defeated by the Byzantines at the village of Motah south of Kerak in Jordan. In this battle the Arabs lost some of their most able leaders. The situation was soon reversed, however, and in the year 636 c.e. the Arab armies defeated a major Byzantine force near the Yarmuk River.

This was a victory that would transform life west and east of the Jordan River. Not only did major changes now begin to occur in the architecture of Palestine, but settlement patterns in villages and cities also took on a different form in response to new political and economic conditions. The religion of Islam also had a transforming effect upon the local population. Whereas the churches of Roman and Byzantine Christianity had predominated during the previous six centuries, now as the faith of Islam took root mosques began to appear in many of the villages and towns.

As the first dynasty to rule in the name of Islam, the Umayyads left behind many important remains. Being the first Islamic regime, they attempted to fashion a program of governance based on the Qur'an's prescriptions on social, political, and economic life. Such efforts were not always effective, however, and political corruption and self-aggrandizement characterized the reigns of some of the Umayyad caliphs. Nevertheless, the time was also a creative one, accompanied by a flowering of architecture, art, pottery, and writing.

The recent excavations in Jerusalem around what Jews today call the temple mount and Muslims the Haram esh-Sherif (the "noble sanctuary") show that the Umayyads fostered a great deal of building activity in the holy city. On the south and southwest exterior of the Dome of the Rock, Umayyad builders constructed a complex of buildings, several of which were doubtlessly administrative offices related to the mosque area nearby. Structures such as these indicate that a religious group

Figure 14.2. Old City of Jerusalem showing one of its two market *(suq)* streets.

of overseers something like the modern Muslim *waqf* may have had quarters in these buildings. Members of this group of wardens would have been entrusted with supervising the religious concerns in the holy city. These extensive remains in the sacred area of the city indicate the new role Islam was to play in the development of Jerusalem.

The most important structure dating to Umayyad times, however, was the Dome of the Rock itself, or Qubbat es-Sakra as it is known in Arabic. Built over the mountainous rock on which Abraham (Ibrahim in the Qur'an) showed his willingness to bow to the commands of God in offering his son Isaac (Genesis 22), the Dome of the Rock was constructed toward the end of the first century of Islam. Dedicated in 692 c.e., this octagonal structure is today a landmark of the city of Jerusalem. A second mosque, the al-Aqsa, was built shortly thereafter, although it has been rebuilt several times and today has a form given it during Crusader times.

The present city of Jerusalem, with its two main streets jutting off to form the main passages through the market, derived its character in part from the age of the Umayyads, although the design of the Umayyad city was indebted to the Roman plan of Aelia Capitolina, the city of Jerusalem built during the time of Hadrian (117–138 C.E.). The main street, or *cardo*, of the Roman city and its shops continued in Umayyad times, forming the market area and serving as the economic hub of the city.

That the idea of the Arab market, or *suq*, goes back to the earliest period of Islamic history has been illuminated by excavations at a site north of Tel Aviv called Apollonia-Arsuf. Excavation here uncovered a market dating to Umayyad times. And as in the case of Jerusalem, the Umayyad market street here was apparently influenced by the layout of the earlier Roman town of Apollonia. The excavations at Apollonia have found evidence of Roman remains below the Umayyad town.

In their architecture and art, such as that represented by the Dome of the Rock, Muslim artists and architects attempted to give expression to the beauty and order that they believed witnessed to the divine creator's perfection. The principal belief of Islam, that everything comes from Allah and fits into his design, stimulated the simplicity, proportion, and mathematical exactitude found in a building such as the Dome of the Rock.

Outside Jerusalem, an impressive ruin was the winter palace of the caliphs built near Jericho at a site today called Khirbet al-Mefjar. Besides the extraordinary architecture and mosaic floors of the palace, an abundance of Umayyad pottery also came to light in the excavations.

And finally, the Umayyads built in the eastern Jordan desert a hunting lodge known today as Qasr al-Amra. The vaulted ceilings and walls of this small building were lavishly decorated with frescoes, giving an insight into the secular side of life during this part of the Islamic period. In fact, these frescoes seem at times to contradict a stricter application of Islamic principles in art at this time.

THE ABBASID DYNASTY

Although the Abbasids, who succeeded the Umayyads, created magnificent buildings and monuments in the eastern part of the empire, they devoted less effort to developing areas such as Palestine away from the center of their domain. Significant remains of Abbasid architecture have not been forthcoming in Palestine, despite the fact that Jerusalem remained symbolically important and repairs were made to the Dome of the Rock. In contrast to the luxurious city of Baghdad, that reached its height during this period, Jerusalem was largely maintained in the condition left by the preceding caliphs. Some of its structures even degenerated and fell into ruin under Abbasid neglect.

The archaeological record also indicates that Palestine under the Abbasids had become predominantly a village society, with peasant farmers making their livelihood by working the fields. One example of this was found at Taanach, where excavations showed that the Abbasid occupation was small, and where botanical remains suggested that the settlers were primarily occupied with cultivating the fields of the Esdraelon Plain nearby.

On the other hand, recent excavations have uncovered and restored a town dating to this dynasty on the Red Sea at modern Aqaba. Known as 'Aila, this harbor town played a major role in the economy of Abbasid as well as Fatimid society. Ships plying the Red Sea and Indian Ocean made use of this harbor in transporting export and import products. One of the vessels found among the ruins came from China, which indicates the extent of the commerce carried on. Important were the various constructions at the site, including a possible palace or government building established by the Fatimids. The entire town was surrounded by a wall, with a series of towers sometimes standing more than twelve feet high.

The rule of the Abassids consequently had an impact on life in Palestine. The most common pottery identified in Palestine as Abbasid is a gray ware with corrugated sidewalls, often decorated with white wavy lines. This pottery appeared abundantly in the Abbasid layers at Taanach, and has been found at many excavated village settlements of the ninth and tenth centuries C.E.

Two realities, however, cut the Abbasids off from Palestine during the last two centuries of their reign. One was the Crusades, which placed Palestine under the control of the Christian west. The other was the growing power of the Ayyubid Dynasty that managed to wrest Egypt, Palestine, and Syria from the Abbasids during the last century of the latter's rule.

The final days of Abbasid rule in Iraq were felt in Palestine, but nothing to the extent of what the Mongolian invasion brought on the eastern kingdom. Begun by Genghis Khan, the devastation of the Mongols was completed by his grandson, Hulagu, who sacked Baghdad in 1258 c.e., brutally exterminating a large part of this city's population.

THE AYYUBID AND MAMLUK DYNASTIES

The times of the Ayyubids and Mamluks provided a new impetus to developments in Palestine. The turning point came with Saladin's successful battle against the Crusaders at Hittin in the Galilee hills in 1187 c.e., following which Jerusalem was liberated and the land returned to Muslim control. The reign of the Ayyubids was short-lived, however, and as their power weakened, control of Egypt and Palestine fell into the hands of the Mamluks, also based in Egypt.

The age of the Mamluks witnessed the construction of some of the remarkable architecture of the Islamic period. One prominent remain, called the White Mosque, was studied recently by an expedition that has characterized its main architectural motifs. Located in the modern town of Ramleh, the building's elegant style indicates the investment the Mamluk rulers put into Palestine.

Agriculture during the age of the Mamluks made use of techniques reminiscent of those employed earlier by the Romans, Nabataeans, and Byzantines. New systems of aqueducts were employed to divert water to promising agricultural lands. Excellent examples of such systems have been found in the southern Dead Sea valley in Jordan, where several aqueducts were apparently built originally by Mamluk technicians.

Such water control made possible the introduction of a number of new crops into Palestine. One of these was sugar cane. This plant had been cultivated along the wet banks of the Nile River. It seems that it was under the Mamluks that the sugar cane industry was introduced into the southeastern Dead Sea valley and the northern Araba. As the archaeological study of sugar mills advances, our understanding of the economics of Mamluk Palestine should increase.

Figure 14.3. Grinding stone from a Mamluk sugar mill at Feifa.

Located in areas where cane was grown, the sugar mills (Arabic: *tawahin es-sukkar*) were a high-intensity industry. Local water sources were directed through an elevated channel to fall on an overshot wheel, which supplied the force to turn large grinding stones used to extract the sugar. Also as part of the mill complex were boiling rooms with vats, where the final processing took place.

The influence of the sugar mill industry left a long-term impact on the dietary traditions of Middle Eastern countries. Large amounts of sugar were used in making tea, coffee, and the well-known sweets of Arab culture in this region. The success of sugar production and processing also affected the economy in another way. Sugar became a significant export product in the Mediterranean world, and even farther away. The harbor city of Aqaba ('Aila) on the Red Sea probably continued to serve as an outlet for sugar, as it did for other exported items.

THE OTTOMAN EMPIRE

Although Palestine was neglected during the latter part of the Ottomans, the early centuries of the empire were characterized by some notable achievements. The new age of control of the Ottoman Turks began with the reconstruction of Jerusalem's walls by Suleiman the Magnificent. Several gates of the city were also rebuilt at this time, one of the best known being the Damascus Gate. The old city of Jerusalem today still bears much of the character provided by the architects and engineers of Suleiman.

In order to secure safe travel for pilgrims to Mecca, the Ottomans also began very early to construct a line of forts from north to south along the edge of the desert in Jordan. These forts have recently been surveyed, and their relation to the protection of local water supplies along the pilgrimage route *(darb al-hajj)* has been established as one of the main reasons for the forts.

Recent archaeological surveys in Jordan have shown that development of areas away from the urban centers occurred during Ottoman times. Settlements were built close to agricultural areas along the wadis in the north of Jordan. Large farmsteads owned by a smaller number of land owners tended to promote a feudal system, however, in which a landlord leased tracts to farmers who had to pay a high price to the owner. Sugar cane continued to be cultivated and was very popular, judging from the numerous sugar pots from Ottoman times found in excavations. The occupants of Palestine during the Ottoman period developed a relation to the land that can still be seen in local Arab villages and settlements, although this is passing rapidly as modernization takes over.

As time went on, the Ottomans became interested in other parts of their vast empire, so that they had little vital interest in Palestine except to control it for political reasons. The area was managed by local administrators called *pashas*. In relation to their long history in the region, the Ottomans consequently left rather meager evidences of achievement. Economic interests seem to have prompted them to invest more heavily in other parts of their vast empire.

ARCHAEOLOGY AND THE CRUSADES

Although the entire period lasted only two centuries, the Crusades left a lasting impact on the landscape, culture, and people of Palestine. With the capture of Jerusalem in 1099, Palestine

Figure 14.4. The modern town of Kerak and its Crusader castle.

began to experience a flow of peoples from the west, something never seen before on this large a scale.

The causes of the Crusades are still debated by historians of the period. Tensions between the Muslim majority and the eastern Christian minority were one reason. Another had to do with the pilgrimage tradition that had developed from Byzantine times onward. The accounts of pilgrims being harassed as they sought to gain access to their holy sites easily aroused French, Italian, and German peasants to respond to Pope Urban II's historic call to free the holy sites. But a variety of other economic and social problems were also part of the picture.

Whatever the specific causes, archaeological ruins from the time of the Crusades are numerous in Israel and Jordan. The most prominent remains are the Crusader castles that dot several of the high elevations of Palestine. The Belvoir Castle above the Jordan valley in Israel is an outstanding representative of Crusader construction. Built on the site of one of the most extensive and beautiful views in the land, the various elements of this castle are still largely intact. Other castles in Israel include the one at Montfort near the Lebanese border, and the Pilgrim's Castle at Athlit along the Mediterranean coast.

Outstanding examples of Crusader castles were also built in Jordan. The one at Kerak rivals the Belvoir Castle, and is one of the most impressive in the entire Middle East. The construction of this castle was ordered by Baldwin I, but its history is best associated with Renaud de Chatillon who ruled Transjordan from this citadel. South of Kerak was the castle at Shobak, known as Montreal to the Crusaders. Along with Kerak, Shobak played an important role in the defense of the King's Highway leading to Aqaba.

The castles, however, were not isolated citadels in a country with which they had little relation. A castle like that at Kerak was the center for human activity for many miles around. Villages that developed within a radius of fifteen miles or more from the castle were tied to the castle's economic and political needs. Local peasants produced the foodstuffs for the storerooms of the castles. There were sometimes intermarriages with local villagers, and the offspring of these unions created an element of the population that still exists in the neighborhoods of some of the castles today.

In addition to castles, the Crusaders fortified a number of the older cities of Palestine. One of these was the harbor town of Accho, or Acre as it was known during Crusader times. This strategic port had been captured by Baldwin I. It was then developed into one of the most important Crusader sites of the country, with various administration buildings for the control of the holy land. The Citadel in Jerusalem also became an important Crusader fortification, being rebuilt on the earlier remains of Greek and Roman times. Crusader fortifications have also been investigated by archaeologists at Caesarea, Ashkelon, and Gaza, among other sites in Israel.

Perhaps even more important, because they touched the lives of many more people, were the churches constructed or reconstructed in Palestine during the Crusader period. The most important of these was the Holy Sepulchre in Jerusalem, built over the most important site of Christianity. Although, as we have seen above, this church was built originally in the fourth century, the structure was substantially altered and added to during Crusader times. As it is seen today, the façade of the Church of the Holy Sepulchre is essentially that of the Crusader church, parts of the earlier Byzantine church being accessible only on the archaeologically restored sections of the interior, and at a few places on the exterior.

Crusader church architecture made use of the massive style of building in Europe but also joined this with Middle Eastern influences. In Jerusalem the Church of St. Anne, with its domed ceiling and apse, is probably the most impressive remnant of Crusader architecture in Palestine.

We are not so fortunate as to possess a great deal of archaeological information about the common life of people living in villages during this period, due mostly to the fact that Crusader remains are relatively recent in the history of Palestine and often have been dismantled by recent occupants. Efforts are currently being made to specify pottery types and associated remains in excavations of villages of Crusader times.

The monumental fortresses and churches of the Crusaders stand today as symbols not so much of an easy relation to the land, but leftover signs of an age of intrusion and dominance. Although some local people found it advantageous to comply with the plans of their occupiers, on the whole the local population of Palestine had an ambiguous relation to these foreigners. Many would never forget the massacre of Muslims in Jerusalem and other cities when they were taken, even as Jews were also sometimes victims of the same events. When Saladin defeated the Crusader forces at Hittin in 1187, the local population was no doubt relieved. As the last remnants of the Crusader forces left Acre in 1291, the Middle East and Europe were left with long-lasting influences on each other's culture and history.

MUSLIM, CHRISTIAN, AND JEWISH RELATIONS DURING THE ISLAMIC PERIOD

It is clear, then, that Christians and Jews did not disappear from Palestine during the period of Muslim rule. Although many formerly Christian communities were converted to Islam, others retained their Christian identity. The town of Madaba in Jordan is one example of a Christian town that remained so under Islamic rule. Another example was the town of Kerak that built up inside and around the castle. In Jerusalem Muslims, Jews, and Christians all were able to establish their own quarters following Saladin's reentry to the city. This was in contrast to the interlude of Crusader rule when Muslims and Jews were excluded from the holy city.

The recent excavations at Um er-Rasas in Jordan, mentioned in the previous chapter, have shown how a Christian community in one part of Jordan continued to function under Islamic rule. This did not mean that the Christians did not experience some harassment, however. The obvious defacing of the mosaics at Um er-Rasas could only have been done by Muslim fanatics, and this was troubling for Christians.

The Jewish community also had a reasonably strong presence in Palestine during Islamic times. The city of Tiberias along the western shore of the Sea of Galilee remained a prominent Jewish center throughout the Middle Ages. Northwest of the Sea of Galilee the town of Safed, known by its Hebrew name Zefat, shared with Tiberias the distinction of having served as an administrative center for Jewish affairs in Galilee. Around the Safed area were a good number of villages that were essentially Jewish in their population. Fortunately, the more remote location of the Jewish communities around Safed spared these villages from some of the excessive military actions of the Crusaders.

Although Jews and Christians as minorities had to fit into the structure of a society governed by the principles of Islam, the fact that they were able to pursue their own faiths with the protection of the authorities was a positive feature of this period. The Islamic period thus did achieve at times an openness to pluralism that brought benefits to the population.

Epilogue

Looking back over the journey we have taken, it seems that two things in particular can be singled out in what we have seen. One is that the peoples of ancient Palestine were faced with the challenges of how they would respond to the environment in which they found themselves. Those who lived in the more demanding niches of the land's ecosystems, such as the hill country or the Negev, had to find ways to cope with and survive in these more difficult areas with their scarce resources. We cannot, of course, assail them for decisions they made to cut down the relatively small number of trees that were available, or to carry on other forms of exploiting the land that were to have long-term effects upon the environment. If, for example, settlement was to become possible in the hill country, areas had to be cleared of trees and natural ground cover and terraces constructed. But if terracing walls were left unattended, the rich but thin topsoils would erode off into the valleys, as happened in many cases.

What we gain from the environmental aspects of archaeological investigation are case studies of how delicate the relation between humans and the environment really is. And that should be of help to us at a time when we have learned to look carefully at the ecological implications of our own decisions and actions.

A second matter has to do with the history of confrontation between peoples in this land and in the larger Middle East. At many points in the long history of Palestine, people were unable to negotiate or compromise to find a solution to their common needs in this small region. This also was exacerbated by the fact that Palestine's diverse landscape presented natural obstructions to easy contact, and therefore encouraged regionalism. Often conflict seemed to be the only course people could entertain in trying to resolve their differences. At other times outsiders invaded, leaving the population stunned, and cutting off the possibilities for normal development. Obviously this brought suffering and disastrous loss to the peoples at any one time. Unfortunately, the cultural remains that archaeology studies bear witness more often than might be hoped to these destructive episodes in the histories of the peoples of this land.

But we have also seen a positive side in the study of archaeological data dealing with ordinary people living in their towns and villages. There were times when in this small region a variety of peoples learned to live together. During such times the archaeological record is mostly free of evidence for the devastation wrought by war. Ironically, the work of archaeologists becomes more difficult when dealing with data from periods without major disturbances, since during such periods thin deposits on the floors of dwellings may be all that distinguishes years of living and use of an area. Destruction debris, on the other hand, will usually contain thick ashy layers, sometimes with masses of objects left from the time the destruction occurred. Some of the finest treasures of archaeology have come from this type of debris.

The newer archaeology makes an important contribution to our understanding by challenging us to concentrate on the long haul of peoples' lives, the day-to-day obstacles they faced in keeping their lives and the lives of those around them going. Great disruptions there were which need to be studied, but we shall gain much in the future from this concentration on the more ordinary processes affecting ancient peoples' lives.

Select Bibliography

GENERAL WORKS ON THE ARCHAEOLOGY OF PALESTINE

Aharoni, Y. *The Archaeology of the Land of Israel.* Philadelphia: Westminster, 1978.

Covers primarily the Canaanite and Israelite periods, preceded by a briefer section on prehistory. The book is readable but moderately technical.

Albright, W. F. *From the Stone Age to Christianity.* 2d ed. Garden City, N.Y.: Doubleday Anchor Books, 1957.

An interpretation of the ancient Near East, including Palestine, written by the twentieth-century's most prominent American archaeologist of ancient Palestine. The book contains Albright's far-ranging historical views.

Ben-Tor, A., ed. *The Archaeology of Ancient Israel.* Trans. R. Greenberg. New Haven: Yale University Press, 1992.

Rather technical volume containing up-to-date discussions of the biblical period.

Dever, W. G. *Recent Archaeological Discoveries and Biblical Research.* Seattle: University of Washington, 1990.

A valuable discussion of uses of archaeology in the interpretation of the Bible.

Harding, G. L. *The Antiquities of Jordan.* London: Lutterworth Press, 1967.

Kenyon, K. M. *Archaeology in the Holy Land.* New York: Praeger, 1960.

Moderately detailed with a focus on Jericho, the site to which Kenyon devoted a great deal of effort.

Mazar, A. *Archaeology of the Land of the Bible: 10,000–586 B.C.E.* The Anchor Bible Reference Library. New York: Doubleday, 1990.

The most complete reference work on the archaeology of ancient Palestine. A good source for following up subjects treated in this book.

Scoville, K. N. *Biblical Archaeology in Focus.* Grand Rapids, Mich.: Baker Book House, 1978.

Focuses on major excavated sites relating to the Bible, with discussions also of Mesopotamia and Egypt.

209

Thompson, H. *Biblical Archaeology: The World, the Mediterranean, the Bible.* New York: Paragon House, 1987.
Concentrates on some of the significant work done in Palestine and the archaeologists engaged in it.

Wright, G. E. *Biblical Archaeology.* Rev. ed. Philadelphia: Westminster, 1962.
Although written some years ago, this book by America's preeminent biblical archaeologist can still inspire the reader to think through problems of relating archaeological remains to the Bible.

SELECTED RESOURCES

Chapter 1. Unearthing the Leftovers of Ancient Peoples

Brothwell, D., E. Higgs, and G. Clark. *Science in Archaeology.* London: Thames and Hudson, 1963.

Butzer, K. *Archaeology as Human Ecology.* Cambridge: University Press, 1982.

Forbes, R. J. *Studies in Ancient Technology.* 9 vols. Leiden: E. J. Brill, 1964–72.

Stager, L. E. Agriculture. In K. Crim, L. R. Bailey, V. P. Furnish, and E. S. Bucke, eds., *The Interpreter's Dictionary of the Bible, Supplementary Volume*, pp. 11–13. Nashville: Abingdon, 1976.

Wertheim, T. A., and J. D. Muhly, eds. *The Coming of the Age of Iron.* New Haven: Yale University Press, 1980.

Chapter 2. The Land and Its Resources

Adler, R., et al. *Atlas of Israel: Cartography, Physical and Human Geography.* 3d ed. Tel-Aviv: Survey of Israel, 1985.

Aharoni, Y. *The Land of the Bible: A Historical Geography.* Philadelphia: Westminster, 1967.

Baly, D. *The Geography of the Bible: A Study in Historical Geography.* New York: Harper, 1957.

Burdon, D. J. *Handbook of the Geology of Jordan.* Amman: Government of the Hashemite Kingdom of Jordan, 1959.

France, P. *An Encyclopedia of Bible Animals.* London: Croom and Helms, 1986.

Hareuveni, N. *Nature in Our Biblical Heritage.* Trans. H. Frenkley. Kiryat Ono, Israel: Neot Kedumim, 1980.

May, H. G. *Oxford Bible Atlas.* Rev. ed. by J. Bartlett. London: Oxford, 1984.

Wolf, C. U. Eusebius of Caesarea and the Onomasticon. *Biblical Archaeologist* 27 (1964): 66–96.

Zohary, M. *Plants of the Bible.* Tel Aviv: Sadan Publishing House, 1982.

Bibliography

Chapter 3. Finding How Old Things Are

Aurenche, O., J. Evin, and F. Hours. *Chronologies in the Near East: Relative Chronologies and Absolute Chronology 16,000–4,000 B.P.* BAR International Series 379 (i), 1987.

Fleming, S. *Dating in Archaeology: A Guide to Scientific Techniques.* London: J. M. Dant and Sons, 1976.

Kitchen, K. A. The Basis of Egyptian Chronology in Relation to the Bronze Age. In P. Åström, ed., *High, Middle or Low? Acts of an International Colloquium on Absolute Chronology held in Gothenburg 20–22 August 1987*, pp. 37–55. Gothenburg: P. Åströms Forlag, 1987.

Thiele, E. R. *The Mysterious Numbers of the Hebrew Kings: A Reconstruction of the Chronology of the Kingdoms of Israel and Judah.* Rev. ed. Grand Rapids, Mich.: Eerdmans, 1965.

Wente, E. F., and C. C. Van Siclen III. A Chronology of the New Kingdom. *Studies in Honor of George R. Hughes.* Studies in Ancient Oriental Civilizations No. 39. Chicago: The Oriental Institute, 1976.

Chapter 4. The Stone Age Occupants

Anati, E. *Palestine before the Hebrews: A History from the Earliest Arrival of Man to the Conquest of Canaan.* New York: Knopf, 1963.

Bar-Yosef, O. Research on Stone Age Archaeology in Israel since 1948. In H. Shanks and B. Mazar, eds., *Recent Archaeology in the Land of Israel*, pp. 3–16. Washington, D.C.: Biblical Archaeology Society, 1984.

Childe, V. G. *New Light on the Most Ancient East.* New York: Grove, 1957.

Garrod, D. *The Stone Age of Mount Carmel.* Oxford: Clarendon Press, 1937–39.

Mellaart, J. *The Neolithic of the Near East.* New York: Scribner's, 1975.

Oakley, K. P. *Man the Tool-Maker.* Chicago: University of Chicago Press, 1972.

Simmons, A. H., I. Koehler-Rollefson, G. O. Rollefson, R. Mandel, and Z. Kafafi. 'Ain Ghazal: A Major Neolithic Settlement in Central Jordan. *Science* 240 (1988): 35–39.

Ucko, P. J., and G. W. Dimbleby, eds. *The Domestication and Exploitation of Plants and Animals.* Chicago: Aldine Publishing Co., 1969.

Chapter 5. Life in the Early Villages

Bar-Adon, P. *The Cave of the Treasure: The Finds from the Caves in Nahal Mishmar.* Jerusalem: Israel Exploration Society, 1980.

Epstein, C. A New Aspect of Chalcolithic Culture. *Bulletin of the American Schools of Oriental Research* 229 (1978): 27–45.

Levy, T. E. The Chalcolithic Period. *Biblical Archaeologist* 49 (1986): 82–108.

Redman, C. *The Rise of Civilization: From Early Farmers to Urban Society in the Ancient Near East.* San Francisco: W. H. Freeman, 1978.

Vaux, R. de. Palestine during the Neolithic and Chalcolithic Periods. In I. E. S. Edwards, C. J. Gadd, and N. G. L. Hammond, eds. *The Cambridge Ancient History* 1, Pt. 1, pp. 498–538. 3d ed. Cambridge: University Press, 1970.

Chapter 6. The First Age of Cities

Amiran, R. The Beginnings of Urbanization in Canaan. In J.A. Sanders, ed., *Near Eastern Archaeology in the Twentieth Century: Essays in Honor of Nelson Glueck*, pp. 83–100. Garden City, N.Y.: Doubleday, 1970.

Harlan, J. The Garden of the Lord: A Plausible Reconstruction of Natural Resources in Southern Jordan in Early Bronze Age. *Paléorient* 8 (1984): 71–78.

Rast, W. E. Bronze Age Cities along the Dead Sea. *Archaeology* 40 (1987): 42–49.

Richard, S. The Early Bronze Age: The Rise and Collapse of Urbanism. *Biblical Archaeologist* 50 (1987): 22–44.

Ucko, P., R. Tringham, and G. W. Dimbleby. *Man, Settlement and Urbanism: Proceedings of a Meeting of the Research Seminar in Archaeology and Related Subjects Held at the Institute of Archaeology, London University.* London: Duckworth, 1972.

Chapter 7. The Second Age of Cities

Aharoni, Y. Nothing Early and Nothing Late: Re-writing Israel's Conquest. *Biblical Archaeologist* 39 (1976): 55–76.

Albright, W. F. The Role of the Canaanites in the History of Civilization. In G. E. Wright, ed., *The Bible and the Ancient Near East: Essays in Honor of William Foxwell Albright*, pp. 328–62. Garden City, N.Y.: Doubleday, 1961.

Bartlett, J. R. *Jericho.* Grand Rapids, Mich.: Eerdmans, 1982.

Dever, W. G. The Middle Bronze Age: The Zenith of the Urban Canaanite Era. *Biblical Archaeologist* 50 (1987): 148–77.

Johnston, R. H. The Biblical Potter. *Biblical Archaeologist* 37 (1974): 86–106.

Leonard, A., Jr. The Late Bronze Age. *Biblical Archaeologist* 52 (1989): 4–39.

Yadin, Y. *Hazor: Rediscovery of a Great Citadel of the Bible.* New York: Random House, 1975.

Chapter 8. Two Peoples Contending for the Land

Dothan, T. *The Philistines and Their Material Culture.* Jerusalem: Israel Exploration Society, 1982.

————. Ekron of the Philistines Part I: Where They Came From, How They Settled Down and the Place They Worshipped In. *Biblical Archaeology Review* 16 (1990): 26–36.

Finkelstein, I. *The Archaeology of the Israelite Settlement.* Jerusalem: Israel Exploration Society, 1988.

Fritz, V. Conquest or Settlement: The Early Iron Age in Palestine. *Biblical Archaeologist* 50 (1987): 84–100.

Gitin, S. Ekron of the Philistines Part II: Olive-oil Suppliers to the World. *Biblical Archaeology Review* 46 (1990): 33–42, 59.

Gottwald, N. *The Tribes of Yahweh: A Sociology of the Religion of Liberated Israel.* Maryknoll, N.Y.: Orbis Books, 1979.

Lapp, P. W. The Conquest of Palestine in the Light of Archaeology. *Concordia Theological Monthly* 38 (1967): 283–300.

Meyers, C. *Discovering Eve: Ancient Israelite Women in Context.* New York: Oxford University Press, 1988.

Sandars, N. K. *The Sea Peoples: Warriors of the Ancient Mediterranean, 1250–1150 B.C.* New York: Thames and Hudson, 1985.

Silberman, N. A. Who Were the Israelites? *Archaeology* 45 (1992): 22–30.

Chapter 9. The Birth of the Israelite Nation

Dever, W. G. Monumental Architecture in Israel in the Period of the United Monarchy. In *Studies in the Period of David and Solomon and Other Essays: Papers Read at the International Symposium for Biblical Studies, Tokyo, 5–7 December, 1979,* pp. 269–306. Winona Lake, Ind.: Eisenbrauns, 1982.

Holladay, J. S., Jr. The Stables of Ancient Israel. In L. T. Geraty and L. G. Herr, eds., *The Archaeology of Jordan and Other Studies Presented to S. H. Horn,* pp. 103–65. Berrien Springs, Mich.: Andrews University, 1986.

Kenyon, K. M. *Jerusalem: Excavating 3000 Years of History.* London: Thames and Hudson, 1967.

Lapp, P. W. Taanach by the Waters of Megiddo. *Biblical Archaeologist* 30 (1967): 2–27.

Muhly, J. D. Solomon, the Copper King: A Twentieth-Century Myth. *Expedition* 29 (1987): 38–47.

Shiloh, Y. *Excavations at the City of David I, 1978–1982.* Qedem 19. Jerusalem: Hebrew University, 1984.

Chapter 10. The Growth and Decline of the Divided States

Avigad, N. *Discovering Jerusalem.* Jerusalem: Israel Exploration Society, 1980.

Gitin, S., and T. Dothan. The Rise and Fall of Ekron of the Philistines. *Biblical Archaeologist* 50 (1987): 197–222.

Kenyon, K. *Royal Cities of the Old Testament.* London: Barrie and Jenkins, 1971.

Shiloh, Y. Bullae from the City of David: A Hoard of Seal Impressions from the Israelite Period. *Biblical Archaeologist* 49 (1986): 196–209.

Stager, L. The Archaeology of the Family in Ancient Israel. *Bulletin of the American Schools of Oriental Research* 260 (1985): 1–35.

Ussishkin, D. *The Conquest of Lachish by Sennacherib*. Tel Aviv: Institute of Archaeology, 1982.

Chapter 11. Persians, Greeks, and Jewish Revolt

Cross, F. M., Jr. The Papyri and Their Historical Implications. In P. W. Lapp and N. L. Lapp, eds., *Discoveries in the Wadi ed-Daliyeh*, pp. 17–29. Annual of the American Schools of Oriental Research 41 (1974).

Lapp, P. *Palestinian Ceramic Chronology 200 B.C.–A.D. 70*. New Haven: American Schools of Oriental Research, 1961.

———. The Pottery of Palestine in the Persian Period. In A. Kuschke and E. Kutsch, eds., *Archäologie und Altes Testament: Festschrift für Kurt Galling*, pp. 179–97. Tuebingen: J.C.B. Mohr (Paul Siebeck), 1970.

Ronen, Y. The First Hasmonean Coins. *Biblical Archaeologist* 50 (1987): 105–7.

Stern, E. *Material Culture of the Land of the Bible in the Persian Period, 538–332 B.C.* Warminster, England: Aris and Phillips, 1982.

Chapter 12. The Coming of Rome

Bowersock, G. W. *Roman Arabia*. Cambridge: Harvard University Press, 1983.

Browning, I. *Petra*. Rev. ed. London: Chatto and Windus, 1982.

———. *Jerash and the Decapolis*. London: Chatto and Windus, 1982.

Holum, K. G., R. L. Hohlfelder, R. J. Bull, and A. Raban. *King Herod's Dream: Caesarea on the Sea*. New York: W. W. Norton, 1988.

Parker, S. Thomas. *Romans and Saracens: A History of the Arabian Frontier*. Dissertation Series 6. Baltimore: American Schools of Oriental Research, 1986.

Yadin, Y. *Masada: Herod's Fortress and the Zealots' Last Stand*. New York: Random House, 1966.

Chapter 13. Jews And Christians during Roman and Byzantine Times

Groh, D. E. Jews and Christians in Late Roman Palestine: Towards a New Chronology. *Biblical Archaeologist* 51 (1988): 80–96.

Levine, L. I., ed. *Ancient Synagogues Revealed*. Jerusalem: Israel Exploration Society, 1981.

Ma'oz, Z. Ancient Synagogues of the Golan. *Biblical Archaeologist* 51 (1988): 116–28.

Bibliography

Meyers, E. M. Early Judaism and Christianity in the Light of Archaeology. *Biblical Archaeologist* 51 (1988): 69–79.

Piccirillo, M. The Mosaics at Um er-Rasas in Jordan. *Biblical Archaeologist* 51 (1988): 208–13, 227–31.

Pixner, B. The Miracle Church at Tabgha on the Sea of Galilee. *Biblical Archaeologist* 48 (1985): 196–206.

Tzaferis, V. The Synagogue at Ma'oz Hayyim. *Israel Exploration Journal* 32 (1982): 215–44.

Wilken, R. L. Byzantine Palestine: A Christian Holy Land. *Biblical Archaeologist* 51 (1988): 214–17, 233–37.

Chapter 14. Muslims, Christians, and Jews during the Islamic Period

Grabar, O. *The Formation of Islamic Art.* Rev. ed. New Haven: Yale University Press, 1987.

Petersen, A. Early Ottoman Forts on the Darb al-Hajj. *Levant* 21 (1989): 97–117.

Prawer, J. *The Crusaders' Kingdom.* New York: Praeger, 1972.

Rol, I., and E. Ayalon, The Market Street at Apollonia-Arsuf. *Bulletin of the American Schools of Oriental Research* 267 (1987): 61–76.

Sauer, J. *Heshbon Pottery: A Preliminary Report on the Pottery from the 1971 Excavations at Tell Hesban.* Berrien Springs, Mich.: Andrews University Press, 1973.

Schick, R. Christian Life in Palestine during the Early Islamic Period. *Biblical Archaeologist* 51 (1988): 218–21, 239–40.

Whitcomb, D. Aqaba. *Annual Report of the Oriental Institute, University of Chicago 1987–88*, pp. 36–41. Chicago: University of Chicago Press, 1989.

Index

217

Index

Index

Index

Index